Robert L Jefferson

Roughing it in Siberia

With some account of the Trans-Siberian railway, and the gold-mining industry of

Asiatic Russia

Robert L Jefferson

Roughing it in Siberia

With some account of the Trans-Siberian railway, and the gold-mining industry of Asiatic Russia

ISBN/EAN: 9783744755177

Printed in Europe, USA, Canada, Australia, Japan

Cover: Foto ©ninafisch / pixelio.de

More available books at **www.hansebooks.com**

ROUGHING IT IN SIBERIA

WITH

SOME ACCOUNT OF THE TRANS-SIBERIAN RAILWAY, AND THE GOLD-MINING INDUSTRY OF ASIATIC RUSSIA

BY

ROBERT L. JEFFERSON

AUTHOR OF "AWHEEL TO MOSCOW," "ACROSS SIBERIA ON A BICYCLE," ETC.

ILLUSTRATED

LONDON
SAMPSON LOW, MARSTON & COMPANY
LIMITED
St. Dunstan's House
FETTER LANE, FLEET STREET, E.C.
1897

To
JOHN KEMP STARLEY, ESQ.

DEAR MR. STARLEY,

Appreciating the practical and sympathetic interest which you have for some years taken in Russian affairs, I venture to dedicate this volume of mine—"Roughing it in Siberia"—to you, as a small token of my esteem.

Believe me,

Very sincerely yours,

ROBERT L. JEFFERSON.

CONTENTS

CHAPTER		PAGE
I.	THE FIRST DAY IN ASIA	1
II.	RUSSIA'S COLONIZATION SCHEME	12
III.	ARRIVAL AT OMSK	31
IV.	A MOST PALATIAL HOTEL!	43
V.	ACROSS THE STEPPE	55
VI.	IN THE OBI VALLEY	68
VII.	IMPRESSIONS OF TOMSK	79
VIII.	THE END OF THE RAILWAY	101
IX.	KRASNOIARSK	120
X.	DOWN THE YENESEI	138
XI.	AN EXCITING ADVENTURE	152
XII.	NEARING THE CHINESE FRONTIER	166
XIII.	IN THE SYANSK MOUNTAINS	181
XIV.	SIBERIAN GOLD-MINING	195
XV.	LIFE AT THE MINE	210
XVI.	A TRIP INTO CHINA	224
XVII.	LOOKING WESTWARD	241

LIST OF ILLUSTRATIONS

	TO FACE PAGE
PORTRAIT OF THE AUTHOR	*Frontispiece*
SKETCH MAP OF THE AUTHOR'S ROUTE	1
A TRAIN ON THE TRANS-SIBERIAN RAILWAY	8
EMIGRANTS AT CHELABINSK	16
OMSK	40
A STATION ON THE SIBERIAN RAILWAY	64
TOMSK	80
KRASNOIARSK FROM THE RIVER	112
THE YENESEI RAPIDS—SUMMER	136
ON THE YENESEI—SUMMER	160
MINUSINSK	168
KARATUSKI	176
GOLD-MINING APPARATUS ON THE UPPER YENESEI ...	192
TRIBUTE WORKERS IN THE SYANSK GOLD-MINES ...	208
OUR CAMP IN THE MOUNTAINS	224
A GOLD-MINE ON THE TOP OF THE SYANSK MOUNTAINS	240

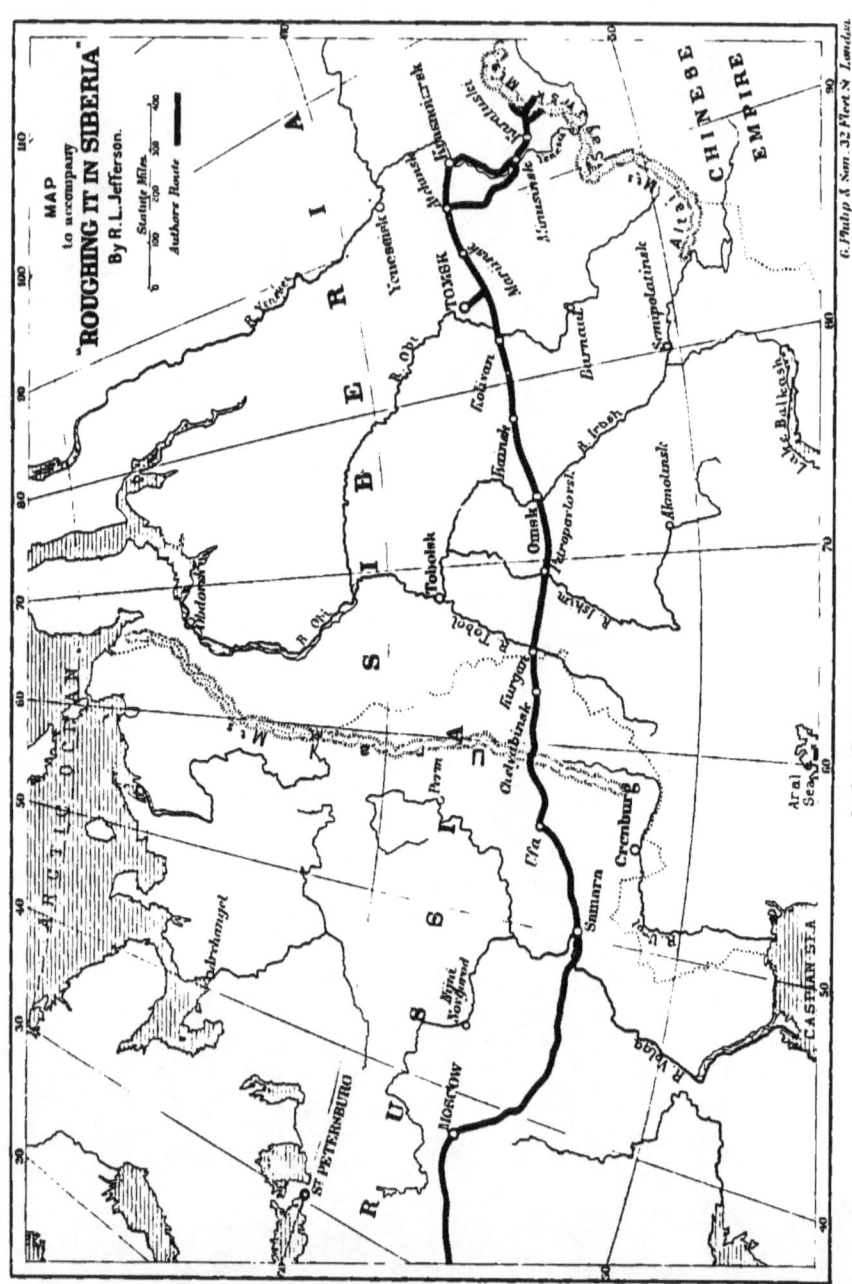

ROUGHING IT IN SIBERIA

CHAPTER I.

THE FIRST DAY IN ASIA.

THE short winter day was waning when the Chelabinsk train, seven days out of Moscow, sluggishly passed the big stone erected in a defile in the centre of the Ural mountain range, and which marked the geographical boundary of Europe and Asia. Since yesterday, when we had left the level plains of Eastern Europe for the uplands of the Urals, the pace had been tantalizingly miserable. Some people say that man can get accustomed to anything, but it absorbs an enormous amount of patience in getting accustomed to Russian railway travelling; the further eastward one goes, the slower becomes the pace, the longer the stoppages at insignificant stations, and the greater the demonstration—beating of tin cans, blowing of whistles, and ringing of bells—which accompanies each arrival and departure. But now, with Europe behind, the whole wealth of Asia before one, combined with the uncertainty of the unknown, and which was backed up by popular prejudice and travellers' romantic tales, the thinking man has food for reflection, and much of it.

We were rounding curves, sharp ones too, on a badly ballasted track, that caused the heavy Russian cars to oscillate alarmingly, notwithstanding the crawl at which we were proceeding. The views to be obtained from the carriage windows were superb, in spite of the wintry aspect which everything bore. It was January—time of deep snow, frozen rivers, and biting atmosphere—everything around (except the interior of the car) was wintry to the last degree. Snow piled up in great drifts on the sharp spurs of the mountainside; the branches of the melancholy birches bowing down with the weight of their snowy covering; icicles hanging in the crevices of the rocks, where, in summer, splashed a mountain cascade. Deep below us, in a narrow gorge, lay the tortuous course of a fast-flowing river, but now frozen to its very bed, and its surface cut and streaked by the runners of many sledges. Now and again we could catch a glimpse of some woodman's hut perched up on the hillside—a veritable house of snow, and as cold and bleak-looking as any one could think to see.

Hurtling violently around the corner, we pass a level-crossing, where stands a caravan of patient horses waiting to cross, with white frost hard on their shaggy coats, and icicles from their eyes and nostrils; a sheepskin-clad moujik, with fur hat over eyes and ears, and feet encased in huge felt boots, complacently puffing at a stunted *papiros*. Here, too, an old woman comes out to flag the train—a woman who looks, from the amount of heavy clothing she wears, more like an animated beer barrel than a human being, and on whose stolid visage is nothing except an expression of tremendous importance at the position she occupies in the service of His Imperial Majesty Czar Nicholas the Second.

Darkness fell; my three companions were asleep. The conductor came and inserted in glass boxes at each end of the long car two diminutive candle-ends, the wicks of which he lighted laboriously. He looked at the thermometer to see how far off roasting we were, and then, after gazing superciliously around, left us. The heat in the car was fearful, beads of perspiration stood out on the faces of my sleeping companions, and yet this is only the Russian way of doing things. The Réaumur glass outside showed thirty-six degrees below freezing-point; inside, the heat was sufficient to almost roast one. And thus for seven days had we sat and lounged, talked and read, and stewed gradually, with no greater diversion than the rush for the buffet at each station, an occasional row with some blustering traveller who would hustle us for places, or the periodical breaking down of the locomotive, which event occurred about once a day on an average.

It was impossible to read, for the light in the car was so dim that one could scarcely see a couple of yards away. The train jolted and groaned and jarred, the candles flickered and guttered, people in the adjoining berths snored, a child was wailing dismally at the other end of the carriage; the heat became more intolerable, and I thanked Heaven when, two hours after darkness had fallen, the creaking of brakes and the distant ringing of bells announced our immediate arrival at Chelabinsk —the terminus of the European system of the Russian State Railways.

The arrival of a train at a Russian station is attended with an amount of excitement which it is hard to associate with the usually stolid Russian. Particularly is this so in Eastern

Russia, where railways are new and interesting. As the train slowly steams in, the assembled mob of sightseers and officials raise shouts of welcome—at least they seem to be. A man hard by the ticket-office performs a terrific tintinabulation on a large suspended bell. All the conductors blow whistles, while the locomotive syren goes off in spasmodic squealings. Slowly, but with many jerks and much grinding, the train comes to a standstill. But the passengers are not allowed to descend all at once. First of all the engine-driver must get off and shake hands with the first half-dozen men that happen to be hanging about near, no doubt receiving in return a sort of congratulatory address to the effect that he has got so far safely. Half a dozen gaily caparisoned policemen, in red hats with white cockades, and armed to the teeth with revolvers and swords, parade up and salute gravely. All the conductors get off—there seems to be quite a crowd of them. All salute a red-hatted, despotic-looking individual, who is gazing about with tremendous scorn and indifference, as if this sort of thing was very boring, although ten to one his heart is thumping with pride and excitement; for he is the stationmaster, salary one hundred pounds a-year, princely for him, indeed. This individual, on thoroughly satisfying himself that beyond the possibility of the remotest doubt the train is really there, raises his hand as if he were about to pronounce a benediction, and instantly there belches from the heart of the mob a smaller mob of much-bewhiskered men in white aprons. These are the porters. These gentlemen throw themselves upon the train in a frenzy of hurry; tear open the doors, push, scramble, and fall over each other in their endeavours to get in first, and ultimately disappear from view. The crowd outside grows silent in expectancy; but the racket which proceeds from inside the train tells eloquently that the porters are doing their fell work. The cars now begin to disgorge boxes and men, bundles and women, baskets and babies, everything mixed up, everybody talking. The crowd outside parts, and the crowd *just* out slides over the slippery platform in a hard mass to the buffet doors. These always open outwards, and are generally just wide enough for a thin man to get in sideways. Then the crush commences. You are in the middle of the crowd with a corner of a box in your ear and four men standing on your feet. You worm and edge your way out of reach of the box and run your chest against the side of a kettle, blacker than the blackest hat, and which is tied around the neck of an evil-smelling moujik in front of you. Somehow the door gets open; the janitor inside scuttles, in order to prevent being swept off his feet. In we squeeze, and find ourselves in a long white-washed apartment, heated to a suffocating degree.

Down the centre of the apartment runs a long table covered with glasses, plate, and cutlery. Over on one side is a long bar, covered with smaller glasses and large bottles,

A TRAIN ON THE TRANS-SIBERIAN RAILWAY.

[*To face page* 8.

mostly containing vodki, as well as at least half a hundred dishes of the *hors d'œuvre* style—sardines, bits of sausage, sprats, caviare, sliced cucumber, pickled mushrooms, artful dabs of cheese, raw radishes, smoked herring, and such like. For the nonce the crowd ignores the long table, equally so a kitchen-like arrangement in the corner where steams a heterogeneous mass of cutlets and "Russian" beef-steaks, and which is presided over by a couple of marvellously clean-looking men who are rigged out *à la chef*. Vodki is the lodestone of the arrived passengers. Each man gulps down a small glass of the fiery liquid, seizes a piece of fish, or sausage, or cheese, or whatever he may fancy or may be handy, and subsides to the big table, chewing vigorously. Energetic waiters pounce upon him, lay before him a big plate of the universal "stche," or cabbage soup, over which our Russian hangs his head and commences ladling away, apparently oblivious to its boiling heat or the feelings of the people around. The tables fill up. Great slabs of brown meat, floating in fat, are distributed with rapidity, and which are with equal rapidity demolished. Manners are delightfully absent. People jostle, growl, and gulp; smoke *papiros* and puff the smoke in each other's faces; or make the most disgusting noises with their mouths. At last, having got through several pounds of meat and fat, and drunk about six to eight glasses of lemon-coloured hot water, which is called tea, per man, the crowd lounges around in contentment, and waits patiently for the bell to announce the probable departure of the train—which may be anything in the region of one hour to four, or while there is a bit of food in the buffet uneaten.

What a relief to get out of such an evil-smelling mob and the heat and general nauseating surroundings, and, wrapt warmly in furs, to promenade the ice-covered platform! They have unscrewed the engine from the cars, and it has disappeared into the blackness of night on a search for wood and water.

At one end of the platform the third and fourth class passengers, peasants of the humblest order, are huddled together—sitting or lying, some asleep, some laughing boisterously—a group of girls in their midst crooning forth a wailing song to the accompaniment of a harmonica, the national musical instrument of the Russian moujik. Over to the left, twinkling lights denote the town of Chelabinsk. Eastward all is black, save for the blinking of a signal light a mile away. That is the road to Siberia, and here is the commencement of the Trans-Siberian Railway.

CHAPTER II.

RUSSIA'S COLONIZATION SCHEME.

I haven't yet introduced you to my companions. Thomas Gaskell, citizen of the United States of America, short, fair, a little bit bald, with a record of having travelled through the whole of Asia from end to end, and still only twenty-eight years of age. John Scawell, British subject, tall, dark, reserved, and just fresh from Western Australia, India, and the Transvaal. Evan Asprey, also British subject and also slightly bald, medium height, fair and good to keep close to, as he had already spent five years in Siberia, and was the only one amongst us who understood clearly more than twenty words of Russian. Here we were, then, at the commencement of Siberia, and bound to one of the wildest regions of that wild country—the Syansk Mountains on the Chinese frontier. Our mission was one entirely of peace, although the customs officials at the Russian frontier *had* confiscated Scawell's Mannlicher rifle and Webley revolver, and might have done the same with my Smith and Wesson, if I hadn't had it up my sleeve at the time. We were going out just to see what Siberia was like. Half pleasure, half business. People at home thought Siberia was a land of promise. The Trans-Siberian Railway was opening the country. Germans with a loose eye for business had announced their intention of looking up Asiatic Russia. Being English, we wanted to get in also—if not the first, at least in the van.

The station at Chelabinsk was not a cheerful place to spend six hours in—for that was the amount of time which had to lapse ere the train bound for Kreveschokovo on the banks of the river Obi was billed to leave.

Gratuitous information concerning the Trans-Siberian Railway was freely offered by fellow-passengers, and we began to fear the worst. Tales about three hours' stoppages at small stations; half a day here and a day there. No bridges over the Obi and Chulim rivers; so that the monotonous train journey should be relieved by a little sledging. An affable man is the Russian traveller, and a cheerful liar. The Russian for "I know" and "I *don't* know" are so nearly alike that only a Russian can tell the difference, and maybe this is why he would rather tell an untruth than confess ignorance. Beneath his affability, however, the observer can easily detect a purpose. His soul-absorbing desire is to know who and what you are, where from, where going to, and what you are going to do. What do you think of Russia? How old are you? Will England let Russia have Constantinople? How many millions of roubles have you got? Have you seen absolutely the finest city, and the finest street in the world—St. Petersburg and the

Nevsky Prospect respectively? If one is wise he will be frank. But the torrent of reiterated questions at every fresh acquaintance becomes boring after a bit, and oftentimes we preferred to keep in our bunks in the train rather than be compelled to go over the jargon of stereo-typed replies in the buffet. English is almost unknown in this region of the Urals; next to Russian, German seems the language most freely spoken. Military officers and function-aries of upper rank know French, but English we never heard spoken in all our railway journey from Moscow. I think that some-times we were looked upon as curiosities, if one might judge from the number of glances and finger points directed towards us, and the oft-repeated word "Anglichiny," or "Englishman," when circumstances compelled us to declare our nationality. But I must say that though they were inquisitive we were invariably treated with respect by our fellow-travellers.

But on one occasion, three overbearing

Russian functionaries, who are revered as Chinovniks, tried to take advantage of our slim knowledge of things Siberian. The Russian cars, I might say, by way of preface, are built on the side-corridor principle; each *coupé* is designed to hold four persons— two on racks, which are formed by lifting up the back of each seat and securing them by means of iron outswinging tee-pieces, and two on the main seats themselves. We had liberally bribed our porter to get us a complete *coupé*, but it was while we were partaking of a last glass of tea in the buffet that the three Chinovniks referred to, being probably dissatisfied with their own quarters, removed our baggage and installed themselves in our places. One of us had slipped out of the buffet to see that nothing was being stolen, and brought back the dismal news. There was scant hope of our getting justice, but we awaited our opportunity. Thinking themselves safe, the Chinovniks could not resist the fascination of tea-drinking, and their

EMIGRANTS AT CHELJABINSK.

departure was a signal for a combined attack on their baggage, its removal, and the replacement of our own. The Chinovniks returned as the train was on the point of leaving. They glared at us. We gazed blandly back. They spoke loudly and long to us. We replied by unrolling our blankets and pillows and preparing for slumber. They raved at us; but we only looked at them with mild reproach. They fetched the conductor, who, after listening to their tale, which was shouted with three voices in his two ears, addressed a question to us, which to three of the four, at any rate, was as incomprehensible as Afghan or Volapuk. We could only fall back upon our standard saviour, and that was to cry simultaneously, "*Neo panimio paa Ruski!*"—"I don't understand Russian!" The conductor shrugged his shoulders and looked inquiringly at the Chinovniks. The Chinovniks raised their voices in their great ire, and then the conductor did absolutely the wisest thing he could, and that was to leave the car. The Chinovniks were nonplussed, vocal persuasion had utterly failed to move us; forcible was entirely out of the question for a Russian, and so they had to leave us.

This little incident may serve as some illustration of the Russian character. I have seen two men in a car, one at each end, quarrelling in the most terrible manner, hurling invectives at each other and boiling over with rage, but never getting one inch nearer one to the other. A tenth of the inducement would be enough for a free fight in England.

It was in the early hours before the Siberian train crawled slowly out of Chelabinsk station and commenced to bump miserably over the badly laid road. The boy-stoker at the stove end of the car commenced his infernal work, and in half an hour the temperature was something abominable. The heat was bad enough, but as the car contained some twenty-four passengers, and all possessed a large number of damp furs, in all conditions of cleanliness, and possessing all varieties of odour, the atmosphere was one almost unbearable. The worst of it is, that the passengers abhor ventilation of the slightest degree. In the roof of the car there is a ventilator, but it is always tightly closed. The windows are double and immovable; the doors at each end are double, one being closed before the other is opened; and thus, day in and day out, scarcely a breath of fresh air can enter the carriage. Inside we sweated and gasped for breath; the instant we alighted at a station our hair, moustache, beard, and eyelashes would become covered with hard white frost, and the exhalations from our lungs would be converted into fine snow.

When morning came, and we arose from our uncomfortable couch, it was to find the train jolting slowly over a level stretch of country; quite uncultivated, and with here and there a melancholy clump of stunted birch trees. We were on the edge of the great Tartar steppe, which stretched north and south for thousands of miles, and which is bounded on the east by the Irtish River, from whose banks stretches eastward Siberia's longest steppe—the Baraba, home of the Khirghiz hordes. The Urals were completely out of sight, and we had the not very cheerful prospect of a fifteen-hundred-mile journey over an absolute desert. Seen in the summer, the steppe lands are by no means displeasing, although their monotony is trying. Instead of the inevitable snow which now stretched in all its glaring whiteness before us, the steppe is a carpet of variegated bloom. The grass is stunted; not nearly as long as that of the American prairie, this probably owing to the fact that much of the water in the plains is strongly impregnated with alkali. These steppes are, with the exception of the vast plains of perpetually frozen ground adjacent to the arctic circle, the most unpopulated part of all Siberia. Beyond the few miserable villages which occur every thirty or forty miles, there is no sign of life except the occasional kibitka of the nomadic Khirghiz. North or south of the high-road the steppe goes uninterruptedly for many hundreds of miles, roadless, treeless, not a landmark to guide one, swampy, sandy, and unprofitable. Under its snowy shroud the steppe looks better.

Late in the day we arrived at Kurgan, a tolerably large town, with the railway station miles away from the nearest house. Unwilling to take the bread out of the mouths of the horse-breeding populace of Siberia all at once, it would seem that the Russian Government has purposely fixed the stations of the Siberian railroad as far away from the towns as possible, in order to give the great army of drosky-drivers a chance. Kurgan was interesting as being the first point where we saw the debarkation of outward-bound emigrants.

Emigration to Siberia is now going on very vigorously, and not before it is wanted, for the population of Russia, European and Asiatic, is very disproportionate. The nomadic tribes of Siberia, such as the Bashkires, Khirghiz, Tungus, Buriats, Votiaks, Kamchakdales, and Samoyedes scarcely count, so small are their numbers in comparison to the millions of acres comprising Asiatic Russia. The official computation of the population being (including both Russians and aborigines) one man to every five square miles. The first cause of the extremely slow progress in populating Siberia may be set down to its distance and inaccessibility from the congested districts of Russia. The only means of reaching its heart, up till the commencement of the Trans-Siberian Railway work, being by the lonely tarantass or the occasional steamers plying the tortuous waterways of the Irtish and Obi systems. The Siberian railway, however, promises to considerably alter this state of things—combined with the startling facts that Southern Russia is rapidly getting overcrowded. Another stumbling-block to the rapid development of Siberia hitherto has been the great prejudice existing against it throughout European Russia, a prejudice which may be said to be far greater than that among foreigners. For many years Siberia has been the dumping-ground for criminals of the worst class. It has been held up as a Bastille-like threat to every Muscovite. Mothers have for ages quieted their noisy children with, "Hush! or I will send you to Siberia!" And thus every man who goes to Siberia, voluntarily or otherwise, is looked upon as an exile. Although the want of communication may be set down as the first, the chief cause undoubtedly exists in Siberia having been made a penal colony.

It is said that the great famine of 1890–1 which spread throughout Southern Russia, turned the eyes of the Government Siberia-wards as a possible outlet for surplus population. The late Czar had ever taken a kindly interest in his Asiatic possessions, and it was the dream of his life to see Siberia developed to its fullest extent. The wish was commendable, but the means were lacking. It was in order to see with imperial eyes what Siberia was that the present Czar (then Czarevitch) took his memorable journey across the steppes and mountains from the Pacific coast, and then came Alexander's famous ukase: "Let there be a railway built across Siberia—the shortest way possible." The Czarevitch was then in Vladivostock, the Russian Pacific port. A telegram from St. Petersburg bade him remain there and await the corner-stone, which was to be laid in that town as the foundation-piece of what will, in the course of a few years, rank as the monumental railway enterprise of the nineteenth century. Alexander, right up to his death, cherished his colonization scheme, and the heritage he left his son has been energetically pushed forward.

Some assert that the idea which dominated the Siberian railway scheme was that of strategy. While there may exist the strategical undercurrent, no one who has passed over the line from end to end as far as it is constructed can be oblivious to the fact that at present, at any rate, one of the principal objects of the railway is the transportation of emigrants to the fertile valleys of Central Siberia. The train-bound traveller passes train load after train load of outward-bound emigrants. At the principal stations of Chelabinsk, Kurgan, Omsk, Kainsk, and Atchinsk, emigrants by the hundreds are detrained, and may be seen encamped by the roadside awaiting their further transportation north, south, or east. The numbers are evidence complete that the attractions offered by the Government outweigh entirely prejudice and the discomfort of a long journey.

The principle underlying Russia's colonization scheme is similar to England's policy with regard to Canada, only that the means are easier and the efforts and influence more energetic and widespread. The agents of the Government are sent to the most thickly populated or distressed portion of European Russia, and there the desirability of emigrating to Siberia is impressed upon the more industrious of the peasantry, who, in Russia itself, can scarcely make ends meet. Neer-do-wells are not catered for, but the Russian Government offers inducements to the willing, and at the same time fixes a nominal fare to Siberia, in order to keep out the absolute drones. This fare is fixed at the rate of one-twentieth of a penny per verst; and thus it is possible for a peasant to travel, say, three thousand versts (two thousand miles) for the moderate sum of six roubles (13s. 3d.). From Southern Russia this would land the emigrant in the heart of Siberia.

On arrival at his destination, the colonist is given a free grant of land, ten deseteens in area, which equals about twenty-seven acres English. He has permission to cut enough wood to build his house and fencing and to provide him with fuel for one year. Thus, with a clear start, and providing the peasant is industrious and frugal, there is every opportunity for him of not only being able to feed and clothe himself and his family warmly and cleanly, but of making a small profit out of agricultural pursuits. For purposes of comparison, it may be as well to state that in Russia itself the peasant is allowed only four deseteens of land, but, as the price of agriculture is abnormally low, it is next door to impossible for him to make ends meet, inasmuch as the rude agricultural instruments he uses, and the entire absence of artificial fertilization, in a few years impoverishes his property to such an extent that it is hopeless. With the increased acreage in Siberia, a better climate, and a richer soil, his chances are enhanced, while a powerful factor is that agricultural prices all round rank from fifty to a hundred per cent. higher than in European Russia. Of course such prices will not last for ever, but as Siberia, minerally and commercially, is far richer than Russia itself, the peasant is bound to come in for some of the reflected prosperity.

The Westerner might perhaps take exception to the manner in which the emigrants are transported to Siberia. I confess it came upon me at first with a shock. The emigrants' train is simply one of cattle trucks, each car being marked on the side for "forty men or eight horses." There are no seats or lights provided, and into each of these pens forty men, women, and children have to herd over a dreary railway journey of fourteen or fifteen days. They have to provide their own food, but at every station a large samovar is kept boiling in order to provide them with hot water for their tea. At the points of detrainment the emigrants are compelled to camp on the steppe or on the mountain-side until provision is made for them to proceed to the land apportioned off to their use. The filth, the rags, the utter woe-begone aspect of the Russian emigrant is something inconceivable to the European, but then it must be remembered that the Russian moujik is used to roughing it all his life, and to hog, forty a time, in a cattle truck, or to sleep by the camp fire, with no more covering than the sky, is no very great hardship for him.

It must be gratifying to the Russian Government that the privileges offered to the peasant have been keenly appreciated, and the difficulty which now exists is to get the land ready for the overwhelming tide of colonists flowing into Siberia. In 1896 alone nearly a quarter of a million peasants left Russia for Siberia. At that time neither the railway nor the colonizing department could cope with the rush, and the Emperor was compelled to issue the ukase commanding the officials of the various Siberian Governments to drop all other State work and devote, for the time being, their efforts to the colonization movement. For a time things were in rather a chaotic state, and a large number of emigrants, finding no land ready for them, returned to Russia.

Anticipating my journey a little, I had at Omsk a long and interesting conversation with one of the head officials of the Colonization Department. He was on his way to Turkestan, there to confer with the officials regarding the colonization of that valuable and practically un-Russianized possession. He assured me that the rush for Siberia had not only completely astonished the authorities, but was rather startling in the fact that it threatened to deplete portions of Russia of labour. The Russian peasant is of such a simple disposition that he is apt to think the inducements offered him are the means to a comparative paradise. Thus many of the emigrants have suffered sore disappointment, and, partly from this and from home-sickness, have returned to Russia. The Government is, however, grappling manfully with the task that it has set itself, and it will take but a few short years to even up the disproportionate population of Russia considerably. One fact cannot be overlooked, and that is that the Trans-Siberian Railway, apart from its political and commercial significance, is likely to be handed down to posterity as the means by which the riches of the great white Czar were brought to the thresholds of his people.

CHAPTER III.

ARRIVAL AT OMSK.

From Kurgan to Omsk the railroad track passes over a wilderness of snow—a dead level, absolutely devoid of interest. It was a relief even to see at long intervals a group of wooden huts, huddling close together, as if for warmth, in that biting cold; the thin blue smoke curling from their several apologies for chimneys, and the glint of the sunlight on the double windows. Melancholy these villages looked, cut off from the entire world as they must have been before the locomotive came snorting its way along. One pleasing feature, or picturesque feature, I might say, was the inevitable round domed church which reared its height above the ramshackle shingle roofs.

Green and white these churches were, with a golden cross perched on the highest dome, and which shines and glitters for miles after the huddle beneath has merged with the snow and disappeared from vision. No matter how small and miserable the village, no matter how poverty-stricken its inhabitants, the church was ever there, ever resplendent, and apparently opulent.

One fact always strikes the traveller in Russia, and that is the overpowering influence of the Church. Densely ignorant as he is, the average moujik's religious devotion is little better than slavish. One wonders whence comes the money to build and to keep up such magnificent ecclesiastical edifices which predominate everywhere throughout the Russian Empire, and only close inquiry and persistent observation can reveal the truth. From high class to low the first duty of the Russian is to his religion. In every house, from the finest mansion to the humblest hut, the gilded ikon hangs in the corner, before which the devout Catholic prostrates himself twenty, and perhaps thirty, times a day. Before every piece of bread he eats, before every glass of vodki he drinks, he will cross himself and murmur his prayers. I do not fear contradiction when I say that every believer in the Russo-Græco faith wears underneath his shirt, attached to a string or chain, around his neck, a metal cross, put on when he was a child and worn till death, and even until his body has crumbled to the earth in which it lies. On the large stations of the Russian railways there is always a chapel with its glittering altar, its ikons and its burning candles, where services are held daily.

The Church seems to stand even before the Czar, though it must be said the Czar comes in a very good second. Great as is the State aid, the help of the people is undoubtedly the mainspring of the Church's revenue. Time after time I have had it brought to my notice that however improvident the moujik may be in his domestic life, his death will furnish the pretext for lifting the slab of the stove to see how much money he has been able to accumulate in his lifetime for his beloved faith. His blind devotion to the Church is nearly equalled by his discipline as a soldier, and without wishing to detract from his character as a man, I must say that, so far as my observation goes, these very qualities, if qualities they can be called, shows how little removed from a mere animal he is. As a Russian, body and soul he belongs to the Church. As soon as he dons the brown jacket of the soldier, body and soul he belongs to the Czar. It is inconceivable to the Westerner that men could withstand the hardships and yet retain such cheerfulness and such patriotism as do the Russians. Iron discipline, which would make the educated and better civilized soldier mutiny or desert in a week, he submits to with equanimity. Kind words he knows not; ill fed, ill clothed, wretchedly housed, and with seldom or never a kopeck in his pouch, yet he maintains even gaiety in his desolate life. This utter abasement of the man is very difficult to realize, it is so essentially Russian that none but one who has seen it can fully comprehend its significance.

An officer of cavalry once told me a little story concerning the discipline and devotion to duty of the Russian peasant. The scene was at Cronstadt, the island fortress off St. Petersburg, where three officers, respectively English, German, and Russian, were discussing the merits of their men. Each maintained his was the better disciplined, and on the argument growing hot the Russian proposed a test. They repaired to one of the batteries, and there the English and German officers each ordered up one of their men, as the Russian did one of his common soldiers. These men drew up in line before their captains.

The English officer pointed to the port, below which the rocks lay some hundreds of feet.

"Attention! Walk out of that port!" he cried in a voice of command.

The man stepped forward, white as a sheet, but hesitated.

"What good am I doing my country by this?" he asked huskily.

"Stand back," said the officer.

The German officer motioned to his man.

"Walk out of that port!" he commanded.

The German stepped forward, he too hesitated, and glanced appealingly at his commander.

"Will you keep my mother and father, sir, if I do it?"

"Stand back," said the officer.

The Russian officer motioned to his man.

"Walk out of that port!"

The man was livid, but he stepped forward briskly; as he did so he raised his eyes and made the sign of the cross, the next second he would have precipitated himself on the rocks below, had not the officer's iron grip restrained him.

This tale was told me with great unction, as illustrative of the superior discipline of the

ARRIVAL AT OMSK 37

Russian soldier; but I did not care to offend my friend by giving voice to my opinion that the demeanour of the English and the German soldiers illustrated that fact which has so often been emphasized in warfare, that an intelligent preservation of one's life is far better for the cause than blindly throwing that life away.

Bump, bump, bump; rattle, rattle, rattle; on hurtled the train, morning merged into afternoon, and the grey shadows which heralded night came stealing over the steppe. Darkness black and heavy enveloped us. Once more we made up our crude beds, and settled for the night. Peterpavlovsk we reached in the middle of the night, and where we sleepily alighted for something to eat, and participated for the hundredth time in the rude scramble which ever accompanied that procedure. Back to bed again, and sometimes sleep, helped thereto by a concert of gurgling snores, tobacco smoke, and odours of vodki. Morning broke, and for all the difference in our surroundings we might as well have been where we were the day before. Grubby, weary, and profoundly sick of each other's company, since we had told every story we knew, and had long since comfortably settled the affairs of the world in long-continued argument, waiting patiently, till afternoon, when we should reach our first Siberian city, Omsk.

Our literature was long since exhausted. It was useless to play cards, as one man had constituted himself treasurer, possessed all the money, and it seemed a hollow mockery to borrow under such circumstances; everybody voted chess a bore, dominoes childish, while our only musical instrument—a jew's harp—had long since lost its soothing influence. We could only glare at each other and grumble, find fault with everything, and say what ought to be done and what we would do if only——

"Omsk!" The silver-embroidered conductor punched another little hole in our much-perforated ticket, pocketed his tip, and left us to scramble our baggage together.

And even this was a delight. We were to stay over two days in Omsk, and those two days were to be a welcome relief from the seemingly never-ending train journey. Soon we came in sight of the Irtish, one of those magnificent rivers which Siberia abounds in, but now silent and still under its thick coating of ice. The train rattled over the high iron bridge which spanned this noble waterway, and ten minutes later drew up at Omsk station.

I mention the word "station" advisedly, because, as in duty bound, the Russian engineers had put it as far away from the town as they conveniently could—this time they had managed it by exactly three versts, and no doubt considered they had achieved a triumph. What the idea is in calling a station Omsk, when Omsk is two miles away, yet remains to be explained. Nobody that I have asked has been able to give me a satisfactory answer. Whether they expect the town to grow out towards the station, or whether it is out of sheer and simple cussedness, I do not know; I fancy it is the latter.

On the station steps we held a levee with half a hundred isvoschiks, who wanted to drive us to town. Honour there may be amongst thieves, but there is certainly very little amongst Siberian isvostchiks. The manner in which they fought and scrambled with each other in order to get hold of our baggage was highly diverting. They implored us singly and wholly to follow them. Each man held out such inducements that the brain fairly reeled.

"Come with my little horse, dear barins; it is the fastest trotter in Siberia, it is a beautiful dove, and goes like the wind."

"Bah! Do not believe him, barins; he is a liar. His horse is covered with ulcers, and may drop down dead before you go a verst. Come with me, barins. Here you are, a lovely sledge, just painted, but quite dry, and splendid cushions. Think how much money I have spent on that sledge."

OMSK.

[*To face page* 40.*]*

"No, barins, none of these children know the way to Omsk. I am the only one who knows the nearest and the best road. Take any of them you will, and they will go the longest way and over a miserable road, which will bump you to pieces, perhaps throw you out and break your neck, and then what will you do?"

And amid all this flood of eloquence, smothered in furs and loaded down with baggage, we were jostled and pinched and pulled until a white-aproned porter rescued us and took us to the sledge he had selected. Then all the voices died away in a long-drawn sigh; envious looks were bestowed upon the favoured one, who gathered up his reins, gave vent to a sort of war-whoop, fell rather than got upon the sledge, and away we went at a mad gallop down the narrow roadway, scattering the snow right and left, and swinging from side to side in the most perilous manner imaginable.

It took us all our time to hang on, the while

that the fierce rush through the bitterly cold air made breathing difficult; tears forced from the eyes by the cold instantly congealed; nostrils, too, became closed with ice; moustaches and beards hard lumps of hoar frost. With a cold which it is impossible to register on a Fahrenheit glass we didn't, I am sorry to say, appreciate the novelty of this breakneck ride as we ought to have done. In less than a quarter of an hour we passed through the gates of the city and stampeded like fury down several wide streets, bordered on either side by one-story frame houses, and ultimately pulled up with a jerk, which flung us in a heap at the bottom of the sledge, before a low, mean-looking wooden house which a dilapidated signboard announced to be the "Grand Hotel Moscow."

CHAPTER IV.

A MOST PALATIAL HOTEL!

THE Grand Hotel Moscow, in the good city of Omsk, was grand in name only, and we had only to step inside its portals to realize to the fullest extent that at length we were in Asia. Bad as had been the generality of hotels in European Russia, they seemed like palaces beside this ramshackle affair which was dignified by the name of hotel. A few broken and wretchedly dirty stone steps led us into a white-washed passage, which was flanked on either side by low doorways leading to the six bedrooms—all the "hostinitca" possessed. Seawell barked his shin badly by falling over the brick which, suspended on a rope over a pulley, kept the inner door of the passage closed. Gaskell gave vent to an American expression when he tripped over a long stretch of dirty canvas which was lying, as a sort of apology for a carpet, down the length of the corridor.

The proprietor of the hotel received us with the glare of avarice in his grey eyes. We bargained with him at length for merely the favour of a shelter; for that was all we could expect. He gave us a room for the outrageous charge of four roubles (eight shillings and sixpence), and that was thirty per cent. below his original demand. A lovely room it was too! Two rickety, broken-backed chairs, a small square table, and a truckle bed, on which reposed a filthy and suspicious-looking mattress, formed its sole furniture. The floor was carpetless save for a canvas strip by the door. The usual domestic utensils were absent; there was not even a washstand. There was no lock on the door; the windows were immovable; the walls were of beams laid one on top of another, with the interstices filled with moss and hay to keep out the draught. A delectable hotel this, but in nowise worse than the majority of such places throughout the whole of Siberia.

In case my readers may think I am overpainting this description, it may be as well to explain the why and wherefore of this seemingly barbaric state of things. In the first place, up to the commencement of the Siberian railway, as I have explained in a previous chapter, the only means of communication with interior Siberia was by means of horses. Such enormous distances had to be covered between towns that, in order to accommodate the large number of travellers, the Government erected, on the great high-road which pierces the heart of Siberia, stations at intervals of twenty-five to thirty miles. At these stations horses could be hired at rates set down on a Government schedule, but beyond this and the shelter afforded nothing was provided. It was thus necessary at the outset of the system for the traveller to provide everything requisite for the journey himself. In addition to his luggage, the wise Siberian traveller carried his bed, bed-clothing, food, and, in short, everything that he might require, rendering himself absolutely independent of hospitality on the way. On his arrival at a post-station, he asked for, and wanted nothing but the samovar, or machine for boiling water, with which he made his tea. The charge for the samovar is ten kopecks, which equals twopence-halfpenny. No charge whatever was or is made for the use of the post-house. If one, therefore, excluded the cost of horses, the traveller's outlay was wonderfully small.

As the towns contained the post-stations as well as the villages, and as the traveller came provided with everything he wanted, it may be readily inferred that the chances of a hotel succeeding are very small, inasmuch as the average Russian is parsimonious, even at the expense of his personal comfort. With, however, the opening of the country by means of the railway, it stands to reason that a new

A MOST PALATIAL HOTEL!

class of travellers will spring up, and thus better accommodation may be provided. The demand for this better accommodation must come from the foreigners, for the Russians themselves are sticklers for custom and habit, and the finest hotel erected for their use would meet but mean patronage at their hands.

Thus it was that the accommodation we received at Omsk was of such a wretched character. Unfortunately we were not so versed in things Russian as the Russians themselves, and our inquiry for four beds was met with a stare of astonishment. We did not press the matter, however, after one of us had made an inspection of the mattress which had already been provided. We thought it safer to sleep on our rugs on the floor.

And so it was in this city of Omsk, capital of the Government of Omsk, a military garrison, the residence of a general governor, four Englishmen could get no better dinner than hard-boiled eggs, a tin of sardines, and black bread, to be washed down with tea, out of glasses, and made from the steaming samovar. Of course, had we been of the usual run of travellers, that it to say functionaries, we should have probably possessed papers which would have admitted us to some Government residence. Being, however, only Englishmen, we had to put up with what we could get.

And as the time wore on, our love of the place did not intensify. We did not mind the blackbeetles so much as the animals which dropped from the ceiling in order to disturb our slumbers. I think we were all pretty hardened members, but the vermin of that room rather got the best of us. Yet this hotel should not be singled out as a speciality in that direction. Conversation on the subject once elicited a tale from a fellow-traveller who, as well as carrying his bedstead with him took four saucers and a can of kerosene. On fixing up his bed for the night, his invariable custom was to fit the legs of the bed one into each saucer and to fill the said saucer with kerosene —the suggestion being that nothing alive would

A MOST PALATIAL HOTEL!

pass the kerosene without being asphixiated. But even that, said our traveller, did not keep him out of trouble, for these things of life, with a sagacity which one would hardly credit in so small an insect, would make a detour by getting up the wall, on to the ceiling, and then, having accurately poised, drop down upon the victim—no doubt to his extreme discomfort. A painful and disagreeable subject this, and one which I shall not allude to again.

Our ablutions in the morning were performed in what will, no doubt, be considered a highly original manner. Having conceived the idea that the removal of at least one layer of grime from our hands and faces would not prejudice our case in Omsk, the difficulty was to find how this was to be accomplished. Judicious inquiries revealed the fact that at the end of the corridor the proprietor of the hotel had provided an arrangement for the convenience of those who were so fastidious as to desire to wash. This arrangement was nothing more or less than a brazen bowl, about the size of a small kettle, which was nailed on the wall. A knob protruded from the bottom of the bowl which, on being jerked up vigorously, let forth a few drops of water on the hands; and so with drops so obtained we managed with extreme economy to get through the mockery of a wash. The waste and the drips went on our knees and splashed around generally, but as nobody cavilled we were content. Having primed ourselves on eggs, bread, and tea, we felt fit to do the town; so, after getting into our felt boots and our furs, we sallied forth.

Omsk is the second city of Western Siberia, and its population, excluding the large proportion of Khirghiz, has been variously estimated at between twenty and thirty thousand. It is a trading centre, for here the steamers from Tiumen and Tobolsk call, and a large quantity of merchandize is landed or shipped. European goods come through Moscow, to Nijni Novgorod by rail, are shipped then on the Volga and Kama to Perm, by train again

A MOST PALATIAL HOTEL!

through Ekaterinburg to Tiumen, and by steamer once more on the Toura, Tobol, and Irtish to find destination at Omsk, whence they are distributed to the outlying towns and villages of the great Baraba steppe. It has in its time been a very prosperous town, and for many years the shopkeepers, cut off from direct competition, have made enormous profits and amassed huge fortunes. The merchants, in fact, form the only society of the city. All seem opulent; and no wonder, when one considers the prices which are asked for even the common necessaries of life. There is a shadow, however, looming over the fortunes of the Omsk merchants, and that is the Trans-Siberian Railway. None realize this better than the merchants themselves, who see that in a few years they will have to face something which they have heard of but never experienced—competition with the outside world. It is said that the community of Omsk was bitterly opposed to the railway passing through the city. "You will ruin our trade," they cried as with one voice; but the decree of the Emperor had gone forth, and through Omsk went the railway. Ultimately, of course, the city will benefit enormously by being in touch with Europe, but narrow-minded and short-sighted as is the Siberian, it is hard to convince him of this at the present time.

The internal opposition to the Trans-Siberian Railway was widespread, and at Tomsk—one of the most important cities of Siberia—the representations made were so strong that the course of the line (which I am led to understand was orginally planned to take in that city) was altered, and passed in a straight line some sixty miles south. The citizens of Tomsk, however, speedily realized the terrible blunder they had made in isolating themselves from the civilizing trading influence of the iron road. The tide of trade flowing into Siberia passed by Tomsk and ebbed into Krasnoiarsk, five hundred miles further on. Tomsk was stranded, and the doom of the city almost sealed. Representations were made, and a branch line was constructed to connect with the main road; but even this will not repay the initial mistake, and people who ought to know assert that Tomsk, which was once, next to Irkutsk, the most important city in all Siberia, must by force of circumstances sink into insignificance.

But reverting to Omsk, I do not think that it was the opinion of any one of the four of us that it was the most agreeable place to spend any length of time in. A city of wide streets, handsome churches, big Government buildings, and a multitude of frame houses. The governor's palace and the military academy are perhaps the finest edifices apart from the cathedral and the churches, which are always the most handsome buildings of any Russian centre. I had the pleasure of an interview with M. Boulanger, a French gentleman of culture who was head of the academy. He confessed that it was like a ray of sunlight from his beloved France to speak to one who knew his land, for he had lived in Omsk for thirty-five years. I gazed upon him in astonishment. Thirty-five years in Omsk! That dump of houses in the middle of a wilderness! With a seven months' cruel winter! Out of touch with the world! But time had worked its charm, no doubt; he had resigned himself. He spoke feelingly, though, of the land of his birth—for who, be he native or alien, can do aught but love the fair land of France?—and I, being fresh comparatively from the Western lands, could not but sympathize with him in that resignation.

CHAPTER V.

ACROSS THE STEPPE.

But uninteresting as Omsk appeared as a town, it is unique in being the extreme northward point where migrate the wandering tribes of Khirghiz Cossacks. The term Cossack seems to be very little understood outside Siberia or Russia. One is prone to associate it with a soldier, but Cossacks in Russia simply means a tribe that receives special concessions from the Czar for services rendered or likely to be rendered. The Don, Ural, and Khirghiz Cossacks are exempt from certain points of taxation by reason of the military ability of the male members of the tribe. The Khirghiz, for instance, are born soldiers and born horsemen. They look with no uncertain disdain on the Russian moujik, who, poor fellow, is taxed up to his eyes, and who is but a foot soldier when conscription claims him for its own. The Cossack of the Khirghiz steppe is a servant of the Czar possessing such privileges that make him independent of the Russian altogether.

Some few Khirghiz there are who have settled in the various towns of South-Western Siberia—at Akmolinsk, Semipalatinsk, and at Omsk—but the great bulk of the tribe is nomadic. The steppe, which extend northwards for thousands of miles into the regions of Turkestan, forms their home. They move their "kibitkas," or tents, about from place to place, pay no rent, know nothing of taxation, ignore the Russian language, worship Mahomet, live by the gun, and have a good time generally. As a conquered race it appears to me they are exceptionally fortunate; but the Czar, with his far-seeing eye, knows their worth. In time of war and trouble no soldier of the empire is likely to serve him so well as this fierce and warlike horseman.

Next to the Buriats, the Khirghiz are, perhaps, the most interesting of Siberian nomads. The Buriats are Buddists or Shamists; the Khirghiz are Mohammedans. So far as my observation goes, I do not think that they possess the mosques as do the Tartars, but nevertheless they are fervent followers of the Prophet. The vast steppe is their home. They are rarely or never seen in the mountains, but on the steppe, that vast melancholy plain, with its stunted grass and its far-reaching horizon, they live, multiply, and die; their only business, beyond the hope of fighting, being in the breeding of horses, which they sell at ridiculously small prices either to the Government or to Siberian traders.

During my stay in Omsk I had occasion to visit a Khirghiz encampment, and although I had been told I should find them an exceedingly ill-tempered and ill-favoured crowd, I must confess that the reception I received was one which rather prejudiced me in their favour. It was a kibitka on the steppe; three or four tents made of rough canvas supported on birch poles, and with a corral outside for innumerable horses, all hobbled by the hind leg. The tent itself, black and unprepossessing on the outside, was a revelation inside. Gimcrack and gaudy perhaps, but nevertheless picturesque. I can only compare it to the interior of a canvas circus—cut down to small proportions, but of the same shape and possessing much of its gaudiness. Lattice-work, painted a brilliant red, blue, or pink, surrounded the sides. Shields of various colours were hung on the walls, together with festoons of antidiluvian weapons in the shape of knives, arrows, bows, clubs, long swords, and old guns. The floor of the kibitka was covered with the foliage of the fir tree, and in the centre a little raised platform formed the table of the inhabitants.

I went to this kibitka under escort, and was

glad to find that at least one of the tribe was able to speak to me, in spite of the short stock of Russian I possessed. Amiable as he was, yet I detected in the sunken black eye of this nomad the fire of a latent warlike spirit, which needed very little to arouse, and which would make him a formidable antagonist.

The Khirghiz are essentially horsemen, and in the streets of Omsk one never sees a Cossack but what he is riding. What they do, how they live, what is their ambition,—all alike seems more or less wrapped in mystery. The Russian population ignore them, and in return the Cossack ignors the Russian. It is the bayonet of the conscript, however, which keeps them in their place; and it is very rare that they do anything against law and order. Every year the governor of the province will go amongst them, and from the number of their tribe will select one who shall be the headman, and responsible for the doings of his flock for the time being.

Strangely enough the Russians seemed ever

willing to warn us against the Cossacks. They are thieves, murderers, anything you like, according to the Siberian, but when one considers that the Khirghiz Cossacks are merely a conquered race, and that seventy-five per cent. of the Russian population of Siberia consists of convicts, exiled for all sorts of crimes, one is apt to think and compare.

In a former journey through Siberia I had closer acquaintance with the Khirghiz than many men have had the opportunity of. I had slept in their tents, I had drunk their "koumiss," and had eaten with them from the same pot, but never once did I have occasion to complain of their treatment.

We were getting tired of the Grand Hotel Moscow. There was nothing about it which was attractive enough for us to prolong our stay within its shelter. As soon as our business had been completed it was the train again. Back over that dreary road to the station; the same old familiar buffet; the same white-aproned porters; the same officious soldier-policeman, ceremonious conductors, and all-important engine-drivers; the same slow-moving cars; the same heat and smell and general discomfort of those miserable *coupés*.

Our next important point was Tomsk, one of the most celebrated of Siberian cities, and to reach which we had to pass over the full length of the Baraba steppe. We started at night, and the next morning found us out on the great white plain. The snow was deeper here, and the occasional long grass which we had seen on the Tartar steppe was absent. Nothing, look which way we would, was there to relieve the eye. A white plain, a circular horizon—the perspective so deceiving that we seemed ever to be at the bottom of a basin, and ever toiling upward.

We had two days of this, with nothing to relieve its drear monotony but the occasional halt at a wayside station. As we progressed further eastward, so things generally became more humble and more primitive. The stations dwindled down in size and in importance.

The cockaded soldier gave way to a slouching policeman in rusty top boots, brown overcoat, battered sword, and dirty peaked cap. Our stoppages became longer—from minutes they went into half-hours and half-hours into hours. Nobody cared, we drifted on entirely at the mercy of the man who drove us, and, I must say, getting gradually habituated to Siberian ideas. Hurry is a thing not to be dreamt of. We would pull up at a station, which consisted of no platform and but a small hut combining both telegraph-office and sleeping quarters. Food, too, began to get scarce; but the inevitable sardine, and the equally inevitable tea were always to be had. Now and again, at some larger village station, we would almost shout for joy when an unexpected and long-since-despised edible would be placed ostentatiously before us. Cabbage soup, for instance, that nauseating compound which in Russia we had loathed. Now we swallowed it with relish, and smacked our lips in satisfaction. Vodki, too, which we had shuddered at in Russia, we were gradually beginning to think was not such bad stuff after all. Our little party, I perceived, were adopting Siberian manners to an alarming extent. It was the Siberian custom to always take a nip of vodki before eating, but we, being superior foreigners, had ignored this habit. I do not know who started it, but long before we reached Tomsk it was a settled custom amongst us to take that nip of vodki, and sometimes even to indulge in the grimace after swallowing which was orthodox amongst Siberians.

We got careless, we took little trouble now about our beds and our general comfort. Now and again we forgot to wash, and went around dirty, just as other Siberians did. Our boots had not been blackened for weeks, neither had our clothes been brushed, nor had our toilet arrangements been properly supervised. It was hard work to shave on such a rattling train as that, and those who sported the razor in their travelling trunks left it there for days together. It was not exactly wearisome, it was a something which was indescribable, a feeling that prompted a desire to go to sleep for at least three weeks on end and wake up at the end of the journey; but there was no Rip Van Winkle amongst us, and, although we did put in an enormous amount of time in somnolent attitude, Nature was not to be thwarted, and many hours had to be spent in loafing around and in conversational reiteration.

With what avidity we pounced upon anything which would disturb the even tenor of our way! I verily believe that a railway accident would have been welcome; and, once, something very near this did happen, although beyond giving us food for talk and a little healthy exercise, nothing more serious happened.

Bang out in the middle of the steppe, miles from anywhere, the train one day brought up suddenly, and stuck there for three hours. As there was only one train a day, it was hardly possible that we had been side tracked,

A STATION ON THE SIBERIAN RAILWAY.

[*To face page* 64.

waiting for a Siberian "Flying Scotchman" to come along. None of our Russian passengers ventured to inquire the cause of the train's inertion, neither did the conductor, who periodically passed through the train with a face about as intelligible as a sphinx, volunteer any information on the subject. Gaskell and I, however, descended, walked along the line to the engine, and discovered that the tank had burst and the water was cheerfully washing away the track. The engineer was complacently leaning against the buffers smoking *papiros*, his fireman was asleep in the cab of the tender, nobody else was about, and the whole situation was so truly sublime that, being in the condition to laugh at anything, we both laughed heartily.

The engine had broken down, that was clear. How were we going to get on? The engineer didn't know, and apparently didn't care. Had anything been done? The engineer *thought* that somebody had walked along the line to the next station, fifteen versts (ten miles) away, and would telegraph for a new engine. Did he know when a new engine would come? He hadn't the slightest idea. To-day or to-morrow? It was possible, one or the other.

Back in the car we tackled the conductor, and he, too, evinced as much interest in the proceedings as an ordinary sheep does when it goes to the slaughter-stool. The opportunity for a walk, however, was too great, and so, in high spirits, Gaskell and I set off and walked that fifteen versts to the next station. The line ran dead straight across the steppe, and when we had traversed ten versts we looked back and saw the train still standing there, a tiny black mass on the shining metals, with as much life about it as would appear in a prison.

Our energy, however, was rewarded by forestalling the occupants of the train in regard to the buffet arrangements. The stationmaster had prepared quite a decent dinner, and he alone, of those concerned in the matter, seemed to be perturbed at the train's delay. We had a very good time in the selection of the best dishes to be had, and on being assured that there was no possible hope of the train arriving that night, we curled ourselves up on benches and slept the sleep of the well satisfied.

Next morning the train rolled up, and hungry and cursing passengers descended and raided the buffet like so many wild beasts. The over-bearing spirit of the Russian came to the front in all its intensity. They jostled and pushed each other without a word of apology, but rather with a growl of resentment and aggression. And yet not one of all that crowd had been able to shake off the laziness inherited from centuries of lazy progenitors and to tramp the ten miles in order to secure a little food and comfort.

CHAPTER VI.

IN THE OBI VALLEY.

THREE days after leaving Omsk, the train drew up at the rather important station of Kreveschokovo. It was important as a station, because here was the first check in our train journey from the Hook of Holland. We had arrived, as a matter of fact, at the end of the railway metals which lay in one continuous line from the most western part of Europe right to the banks of the Obi River. The bridge had not yet been completed over this colossal water highway, and in order to resume our train journey it was necessary to take sledges from the station of Kreveschokovo, across the river to the station of Ob.

I think that everybody was more or less

glad that the bridge was not completed. To ride in a sledge, after being cooped up in the overheated train, was a bit of a change, at any rate, and I must confess that we four Englishmen jumped at the chance.

We had reached the end of the steppe, and before us now lay mountainous country, and the difficulties which the engineers of the Trans-Siberian Railway had experienced were evident on all hands. The Obi at this point was some two miles wide, and a bridge over such a distance as that was no mean task. The railway, we understood, was completed almost as far as Kansk, nearly a thousand miles further on; but in spite of all the haste of the Russian engineers, the Obi bridge was yet far from completion.

In the gathering twilight of an early February afternoon we stood out on a bluff overlooking the frozen river and surveyed the workings of what must rank as a monumental engineering enterprise. The Obi bridge is built on the suspension plan on high tiers, and is simply a network of girders and stanchions, great earthworks running up from the level plain on either side to a considerable height.

We alighted, and the kind Russian officials left us to shift for ourselves with regard to transportation across the river. We got out our baggage, which was immediately distributed by energetic porters in various and inaccessible portions of the station, and then wandered out to find something in the shape of a sledge which would carry us to the station of Ob, seven miles away. Unfortunately for our plan, the whole of the passengers of the Siberian train were on the same tack, and knowing Russian better than we, managed at any rate to get hold of the best isvostchiks who ply for hire. Ultimately we were able to secure a basket-work arrangement, tied on a couple of runners, and which was supposed to be drawn by a pair of horses, the size of which, in comparison to the size of the vehicle, was rather ludicrous. Whether it is the cold, or whether it is the terribly hard work which Siberian horses undergo, I don't know, but I am safe in saying that the average Siberian horse is not much larger than an English donkey. There was, of course, the usual long and interesting bargaining encounter with the driver of the vehicle. From five roubles we got down to two at length, bundled in our baggage, pushed our way through the crowd of harpies who had looked at the whole proceedings and wanted tipping for so doing, and set off.

Down a little road past the station at a mad gallop; swish! round the corner, and out over a level plateau. We banged against tree stumps which stuck out through the snow, cannoned against fence corners protecting some agricultural property, until, with a whirl and a clatter, we dashed down a short slope and were out on the river.

Before us lay the white expanse of ice, but all hummocky and broken. It is difficult to describe the appearance of that frozen river.

Instead of a smooth level plain of ice, as one would expect to see, the whole surface was one jumbled mass of broken ice, which seemed as if at the very moment of its breaking, it had been arrested by King Frost and frozen solid. Great lumps, ten to fifteen feet high and four to five feet in thickness, towered above us; smaller pieces hung on to the larger by mere strips, and through this wilderness of congealation, a narrow road had been formed for the passage of vehicles. Over this road we galloped at a terrific pace, bumping and scrunching, whirling and swishing, the drosky clattering from side to side, now on one runner, now on the other, and all our traps jerking about like peas in a frying-pan, while we, poor unfortunate mortals, hung on by one hand, and with the other hand endeavoured to smother the mouth in order to warm the air for the lungs. A few minutes of this brought us into the centre of the river, where the ice was clearer, and a level plain stretched before us. It was a sublime sight then to see that noble river so silent and still, and it was something to realize the marvellous work of Nature in having secured the means to that end.

On again, with the light fading away behind us and the greyness of night creeping up ahead. Through the jagged ice once more, until, with a whoop and a halloo, we scuttled over a narrow stretch where the water oozed and spirted between a crack; then up the bank at a mad scramble, to disappear in a miniature forest, to whirl around at a breakneck speed on the edge of an embankment, and to clatter into the station yard at Ob with smoking horses, excited driver, and bruised bodies we, but pleased nevertheless.

The station at Ob is singular from the fact that previous to the Trans-Siberian Railway passing that way the region was a complete wilderness. Four years ago, when the railway reached that far, houses began to spring up with marvellous rapidity, and at the present time it is difficult to buy a plot of land in the vicinity of the station. Nor is this all. Recognizing that the Trans-Siberian Railway is bound to bring a large number of travellers from the East, who will probably in the summer make use of the great steamboat highway of the Obi system, hotels and magazines have been opened in anticipation of that traffic. All this was very surprising to us in face of the extreme apathy which seemed to obtain in every other part of Siberia so far. But the houses in Ob, although constructed of wood, and the magazines and hotels built on the orthodox Russian principle, were at any rate superior looking to those we had seen thus far.

Next day we arrived at the small station of Tigre. It was called Tigre because "tigre" is Russian for "forest." This little station was bang in the midst of the most impenetrable forest I had ever set eyes on. It lay, in fact, in the centre of a clearing—in the centre of a pit, it seemed, for the great black trunks of the pines went up all around and left only a circular space of blue sky visible. When the engine whistled the noise echoed and re-echoed through the still forest. When we looked around, what was there to see? We might as well have been dumped out of a balloon in the middle of an uninhabited land, only that the railway gave the lie direct. A small hut representing the station, a side-track with a few waggons, a glimpse of a house amongst the trees, a forlorn-looking engine-shed away up the line, and that was all—all except that bewildering mass of trees packed so closely together that it seemed as if one could scarcely put one's arm between each trunk—sombre, still, and awe-inspiring. And here, in this inspiriting place, we had to wait no less than nine hours for the train to take us to Tomsk!

Tigre is the junction of the Tomsk railroad, and I have already mentioned the fact that the main line in its neglect of Tomsk has left that town very much stranded. It seems, too, that the Government, resenting the independence of the great Siberian city, has put as many obstacles in the way of travellers thereto as it possibly can. To wait nine hours in a station like Tigre was the sort of thing sufficient to make a man's blood boil— that is if anything could boil in a temperature of thirty-six below zero, Réaumur.

The Krasnoiarsk train departed. We watched it as it drew slowly out of the station and disappeared in the forest, sparks flying from the funnel of its engine and a wealth of smoke mingling with the snow which covered the tree-tops. There were only a few of us bound for Tomsk—seven, as a matter of fact—and we made four of them. Three were Chinovniks, very much uniformed and very supercilious. There was a buffet of insignificant proportions attached to the station, and in this we did our best to while the time away. It was a hard matter, and an experience well to be forgotten, for, with true Russian perversity, the Tomsk train was got ready to start just about the time when we were all in the middle of slumber.

Our natural ill humour was not reduced upon finding that the Tomsk train contained no first-class *coupés*. Some one explained that up to the present the Tomsk section had received no first-class carriages from the works; so, although we possessed first-class tickets, we were forced to put up with the miserable accommodation provided by some old time-worn cars, which by some chance or other had managed to get so far.

The Tomsk section of the Siberian Railway, being, as it was, a something apart from the great enterprise, was if anything worse than the main line itself. It was miserably laid, and the jerks and joltings which we experienced on that ninety-versts ride did not altogether inspire us with confidence. We slept on bare boards in third-class compartments, because the second-class cushions, after an hour or two's experience, became altogether too suspicious for longer stay. So we groaned through the night and woke stiff and bruised, unrefreshed and ill tempered. On we hurtled, at the excessive pace of eight miles an hour, seemingly never coming to the end. Day broke, and passed, and afternoon and its darkness came again. Ninety versts were all we had to do, but what with hours spent at wayside stations, which seemed to have no more importance than one hut could show, we got through time grandly, and, just when it was too late for anything, pulled up at Tomsk.

The usual ceremonial, the usual clanging of bells, blowing of whistles, general excitement, and we descended to shake hands with each other on the fact of having arrived in the very centre of Siberia.

CHAPTER VII.

IMPRESSIONS OF TOMSK.

Our arrival at Tomsk was signalized by the greatest cold which we had experienced so far. The Réaumur glass showed more than forty degrees of frost, and in this bitter atmosphere it seemed impossible to keep up one's circulation. In the miserable drosky which took us from the station to the town we became so numbed that on arrival at the portals of the hotel it was with difficulty that we could dismount. Gaskell was unfortunate enough to get one of his hands frost-bitten, and the thawing of that member was accompanied by pain so intense that he almost screamed in agony. Nor was the hotel at which we were forced to put up conducive to comfort. There is in

Tomsk one very good hotel, called the Europa, but unfortunately we were unable to obtain apartments here, and were forced to seek shelter in a hostinitca, which was, to say the least, decidedly third class—inferior, in fact, to the accommodation which we had received at Omsk.

Bad as was the bedroom accommodation and the general eating arrangements, the hardened traveller could perhaps put up with them, but what was worse than all was the shocking sanitary arrangements of the place—a state of things, however, which is pretty general in Siberian houses. The stench of that hotel was something abominable, a stench carried on the hot air which crowded and filtered into every corner and crevice of the place. All the windows were tightly closed, being constructed on the double plan, with cotton wool in between, in order to preclude the possibility of a particle of air entering one's chamber. To sleep in such an atmosphere was out of the question, and we got out of the difficulty by

TOMSK.

[*To face page* 80.

breaking a couple of panes of glass in the window and tying a piece of sacking over the orifice. That hole in the window, viewed from outside, was something like the funnel of a steamer, the hot air rushing out in clouds of steam to be immediately converted into fine snow. But even this novel means of ventilation did not rid us of the smell, which permeated everything from the door of the hotel to the tiniest room or passage.

The red-shirted and long-haired individual who acted as proprietor and servant combined, intimated that it was quite impossible to get anything to eat. The samovar we could have with pleasure, but of food the only thing in that direction which it was possible to obtain would be black bread. Our supply of provisions being exhausted, and being in a town of some thirty thousand inhabitants, black bread was not the sort of thing to satisfy four hungry Englishmen; so I wandered forth, chartered a drosky, and drove down to the market-place, or bazaar, which turned out to be a big square surrounded by rows of dismal wooden huts in the last stages of decrepitude. Afar off, over a wooden bridge which spanned the bed of a small river, I could see blinking electric lights, and marvelled considerably.

Here was a town which sported one of the greatest inventions of the age, and yet four travellers, willing to pay anything in reason for decent accommodation, could get no better than that of which I have spoken, and no better food offered than black bread! Most of the magazines were closed. A few skin-clad moujiks, muffled up to the eyes, shuffled along in their huge felt boots, and a few horses hobbled at the heel, looked forlorn and miserable by the huge scales which marked the centre of the bazaar.

My driver, on learning by mission, drove me to a magazine, which fortunately was open, and here I was able to purchase a couple of dozen eggs, frozen as solid as stones, a loaf or two of white bread, a box of sardines, and some sweets. The manner in which the eggs were thrown into the bottom of the drosky was a touching tribute to the severity of the Siberian winter.

By dismal candlelight, seated on rough wooden chairs around a rougher table, with the steaming samovar in the centre, we made our meal. Such luxuries as plates or knives we knew not. We carved our bread with a bowie; we held our eggs in our hands, and consumed the contents, not by the use of a spoon, but by jerking all that would come out into our mouths, then breaking the shell and sucking away what remained attached to the skin. For four of us the proprietor had found one spoon, so the bread-cutting bowie served also to stir up our tea. We started on eggs, made a second course off sardines, and had sweets for dessert. Only our perennial good temper made the meal enjoyable. It was not so much that what we had was not satisfying, but the great fact that here we were in a town, one of the richest in Siberia, and one of the most populous, and that it was impossible to get better fare than this.

No wonder that Siberia is looked upon by the traveller with abhorrence. Apart from its inhabitants, no one can say that Siberia is not a land of beauty, plenty, and promise; but it is the nature of its inhabitants which make it the terrible place it is. The independence, the filth, and general want of comfort which characterize every effort of the community serve to make a visit to any Siberian centre a thing to be remembered for many years, and an experience not desirable to repeat.

Yet Tomsk is not without its attractions. It is divided into two towns, the upper and the lower; the latter being on the banks of the Tom, and the former on the brow of the high cliffs which divide the river into two sections. There are some very fine buildings in the city, notably the Military Academy, the Government Mining Laboratory, the governor's residence, the theatre, and half a dozen magnificent churches. The main street is built on the side of a hill, east to west, but the mean character of the houses and magazines on either side, as well as the dilapidated and broken wooden pavement outside them, turns what would be a magnificent avenue into one by no means pleasing to the eye. At night the electric light casts a white glare upon this huddle of houses, and serves to show the unwary pedestrian the pitfalls in the road and the pavement. What this town is like in summer, when the hot sun beats down upon its unpaved roads and serves to accentuate its predominant smell, it is not difficult to realize. Happily for the health of the Tomskite, there is an eight-months' winter, and to this almost perpetual time of frost I certainly think that much of the good health of the Siberian is due. I have travelled in many lands, but I must place it on record that for absolute neglect of the most elementary stages of sanitation the Siberian authorities surpass the efforts of all others I have seen.

Prior to the establishment of the Trans-

Siberian Railroad, Tomsk, being situated at the very centre of Siberia, became the *entrepôt* for the general commerce of the country. Westward, the magnificent water system of the Obi put the traveller in touch with Tobolsk, Tiumen, and the Trans-Ural Railway to Europe. Tomsk was, and still is, the biggest debarking point for European goods. Here, too, are centred some of the great tea magazines, and the residences of several millionaire gold-miners and merchants. Its society is distinctly that of the trading classes. Rich men abound—made rich by the profits of monopoly, but with that monopoly steadily slipping at the present time from their grasp. The gold-miners are, perhaps, the most influential, inasmuch as the industry of gold-mining in Siberia is one in which the Government takes an active interest. They are represented in Tomsk by many of the leading gold-miners of the country, notably M. Siberikoff, one of the richest men in all Siberia, and who has done much towards the improvement of the city. In 1888 he founded the University, the first one, I believe, in the whole of Siberia, and to which, at the present day, students journey from all parts of Siberia in order to complete their education.

While in Tomsk I had the opportunity of visiting one of these millionaire gold-miners, a man whom popular repute said was one of the richest in Tomsk. He possessed, at any rate, the largest and most sumptuously furnished private residence, and was said to be extremely hospitable. And yet this man could with difficulty sign his own name. Forty years ago he had been an ordinary gold-washer in the Semipalatinsk Mountains. That was in the days when gold was found by the handful, when there was very little competition, less Government supervision, and plenty of opportunities for stealing. From a moujik the particular gold-miner I am speaking of became a renter of Government land, and in the course of the next twenty years amassed nearly a million roubles. He purchased houses and land freely in Tomsk, and ultimately became, as I have hinted, one of the wealthiest men in the community.

It is the custom in Siberia when paying a visit, even if it be at ten o'clock in the morning, to go in evening dress. To neglect this is to offer one of the greatest insults you can to the Siberian. Excuses avail nothing; it is a case of being in a land where such a thing is necessary, and if you are unprovided with the customary black coat that is entirely your look out, and by far the best thing to do is to decline the invitation. Fortunately, I was aware of this custom, and had brought with me the necessary costume, and I made the visit at midday.

My host received me with considerable enthusiasm, but although accustomed somewhat to Siberian manners, it was with difficulty that I could repress my repugnance of him. He was unshaven, dirty, and the rusty black clothes which he wore fitted him as a sack would a broomstick. He smoked *papiros*, spat, and made horrible noises with his nose. He invited me to drink vodki, which I did. It was his custom to take a glass, swallow its contents, and then eructate noisily; in which performance he was aided and abetted by several of the male members of the family and some visitors.

Dinner in the house of a wealthy Siberian is a peculiar custom. There is no formal sitting down, to be waited upon as with us of the western world. The apartment into which I was ushered was large, bare, and uncomfortable. An enormous piano occupied one corner; chairs were scattered around on the polished floor; the walls were whitewashed, but without a picture or other ornamentation to relieve their bareness; a great stove, which occupied another corner, sent out radiating waves of heat. Down one side of the room ran a long table, decked out with glasses, bottles, plates, knives and forks, and many and varied articles of food in the way of canned goods. This table was faced by three smaller ones, covered with red baize, and around which, in the intervals of eating and drinking, our host's party would assemble to throw dice or play cards. The Siberian luncheon or dinner occupies hours. You sit around and take a hand at cards or form one in a dice party. Ten minutes elapse, the host comes round, pats each one of his guests on the shoulder, and at the same time flicks his third finger against his neck. This is the Siberian invitation for a drink. The crowd collects around the table, each takes a glass filled with vodki, or with some one or other of the many mysterious compounds which go under the name of Siberian liqueurs, tosses it off, makes a grimace, sometimes the sign of the cross, gulps down a bit of bread and sardine, and wanders back to the card-table.

In another ten minutes a huge sturgeon, smoking hot, is brought in on a dish. The host comes round again, again pats shoulders, but this time moves his jaws convulsively, as if in the action of eating. Up rises the crowd once more, in order to make a combined attack upon the sturgeon with finger or with fork, washing down toothsome morsels with more vodki. Back again to card-playing, and up again to eat or drink—so the day wears on. Conversation is not very brilliant or long sustained. There is a moody, dissatisfied air about everybody—a general, as it seemed to me, want of confidence in one's neighbour—which makes the whole meeting oppressive, so much so that I was glad when the time for departure came, and I was able to get out into the street.

At that moment it is necessary again to observe Siberian customs, this being to shake the hand of the host, the hostess, and everybody who has got any connection with the house, and to thank them for the food you have had; to declare that it is the finest food you have eaten in all your life, that you have never tasted such vodki, and that, as long as you live, you will remember the hospitality you have received. Mine host hurries to help you into your shouba; but you must on no account let him do that, as it would imply that you have not had enough to eat to make you strong enough for that particular office. You gently ward him off and laugh idiotically; he insists, and *you* insist, until ultimately you manage to get into your furs, shake hands again, cross yourself before the ikon on the wall, bundle down the steps into the yard, where dogs snarl around your legs, open the big gate, and emerge into the street.

The ceremony of Siberian hospitality is almost ludicrous, viewed of course from the light of things at home. It is impossible for the Westerner to feel comfortable, and I have it on the authority of a French gentleman who has lived in Tomsk for fifteen years, and is compelled by his position to move about considerably in the so-called society of the place, that he cannot get himself to enjoy the various functions at which he is always an honoured guest.

While in Tomsk, it was my privilege and good fortune to make the acquaintance of M. Shostok, the chief of the Mining Department of Central Siberia, and who probably ranks, next to the General Governor himself, as the most important personage in all Tomsk. I found M. Shostok an extremely agreeable and cultured gentleman, who had travelled much, and was keenly alive to the shortcomings of the Siberian populace. His particular department was one which required a tremendous amount of work, for he was the receiver of all the gold and other precious metals mined in the provinces of Tomsk, Atchinsk, Semipalatinsk, Minusinsk, and Yeneiseik, a district covering many thousands of square miles, and including in its area all the richest gold mines north of the Altai range.

At Tomsk the gold is received, assayed, and smelted, its actual value, less 3 per cent. or 5 per cent., according to the district, being credited to the miner on a six month's acceptance. The average amount of gold received yearly by the Tomsk laboratory amounts to some hundreds of poods, the latest statistics showing 170 poods in 1891, being 7·15 per cent. of the production of the whole country. Eastern Siberia, of which the receiving depôt is Irkutsk, produces far more gold, 1510 poods being the receipts in 1891—63·32 per cent. of the production of the whole country. Considering that Western Siberia is for the main part comparatively flat, the production is looked upon as extremely encouraging, although Eastern Siberia offers greater scope to the capitalist and to the foreign miner.

So far, owing to lack of information concerning the country, and to the universal suspicion attaching to enterprises in Russia, combined with the formidable red-tapeism of the Russian Government, very few foreigners have attempted gold-mining in Siberia; although, from the little that I have learnt of it, I can see that it is as safe, if not safer, to work for gold in that country than in others where the Government itself is not the protecting agent. One thing, however, must be borne in mind : in order to pose as a successful miner in Siberia it is necessary first of all to clearly understand the conditions implied by the Government, and to have a complete knowledge of the language and the customs of the people; for the pitfalls are many, and the Russian Government is not the sort of one to excuse mistakes.

Thanks to M. Shostok's kindness, I was taken into the laboratory, and shown into the safety vaults, where was stored something like two hundred poods of smelted gold. The deep dungeons of mediæval history may be compared to the safety vaults at the Tomsk laboratory. Subterranean passages, guarded by heavily armed soldiers; ponderous iron gates and doors; keys a foot long; rusty hinges, bolts; and all that sort of thing. Four soldiers took us into the store-room, where three enormous iron safes let into the walls glared at us. The locks of these safes were sealed with wax, of which M. Shostok alone possessed the seal. This wax was broken, the safe door unlocked, and there, reposing on shelves, lay bars of the dull yellow metal, representing some millions of roubles and the work of thousands of men for many months.

I had the opportunity of trying to carry as much gold as I could lift, and it was surprising to me what a small quantity it seemed, and yet it would have been sufficient to have made my Siberian journey distinctly remunerative—if I had been allowed the further opportunity of getting away with it. But there were too many soldiers about; far too many revolvers, guns, swords, big gates, ponderous locks, and such things as that, to permit feelings of cupidity even in sight of such wealth. I went out as poor as I entered, except from an intellectual point of view, and proceeded to the smelting-room, where I saw tiny pellets of gold extracted from masses of baser mineral; saw the smallest and most sensitive balance I have ever had the luck to look upon. This balance was so true that a piece of paper was weighed against so many hairs. I afterwards wrote my name on the paper in pencil, and the weight of my signature was clearly shown.

A word now as to the investment of foreign capital in the Siberian gold-mining industry. In England, at any rate, there is, or seems to be, an idea prevalent that before any one can undertake mining enterprise of any sort in Siberia, it is necessary to get a concession from the Russian Government. This is entirely erroneous. All that is necessary is that the intending prospector or purchaser of land shall be rated a good citizen of his particular country. He should possess a paper from his consul or ambassador which gives him that honour. The presentation of this paper, at Tomsk or Irkutsk, to the Minister of Mines will secure for him a Russian privilege-paper, which gives him the right for as long as he lives to prospect for gold or other precious metals in any part of Siberia. He can either break fresh ground or rent or buy existing mines, for the terms of the contract are these:

All the gold he obtains must be handed over to the Government. He must obey in every particular the rules laid down by the Mining Department as to the conduct of his affairs. He is not allowed to have more than five versts of gold-bearing land in any one spot (this in order to give other people a chance). But the Government, it seems to me, in this particular makes one rule and another to obviate it. Thus, although he may not possess more than five versts of land, his son may possess the next five versts, his mother the next, and all his uncles, aunts, sisters, brothers, grandfathers, and grandmothers can go on at five versts a time consecutively, or as long as the money holds out or there is land available.

The penalties for breaking any of the rules of the Mining Department are very severe. It is forbidden to sink a shaft more than ten feet deep without the presence of a Government inspector. Every piece of gold obtained from the workings must be carefully weighed in the presence of the Cossack provided by the

Government, duly sealed, and its weight, value, and venue entered into a gold book. If any mistake be made in the entry, the miner is subject to a fine of twenty-five roubles for every error, and in this particular the signatures of the mining engineer and the mine owner must be attached to the book plain and unvarnished, the slightest flourish or tailpiece to the signature costing twenty-five roubles. Here, again, the Russian system of making one rule to upset another comes in; for all that is necessary to get back the money expended in fines, is to write a letter to the Minister of Mines pleading for pardon, and I believe that this pardon is very rarely withheld.

The gold obtained from the mines must be sent at periods of not more than three months from each other to the laboratory. If any of the gold should be lost in transit, the Government will shut down the mine until that gold or its equivalent value is found. Again, if more than two strikes occur amongst the workmen in one year the Government may exercise its right to close the workings. If one of the workmen be killed by defective machinery, or even in brawling, the works are stopped.

Little things like these may not tend to encourage foreign capital, more especially when above all there exists that autocratic right, which the Emperor reserves, to present you with your passport without explanation or reason, and to give you twenty-four hours notice to leave the country.

So much for the general principles of gold-mining in Siberia. Of the actual detail work of that industry I shall have more to say later on, when, in contact with the rough gold-miners of the Syansk Mountains, I had practical experience of the hunt for that noble metal which has caused some happiness and untold misery for mankind in general.

CHAPTER VIII.

THE END OF THE RAILWAY.

EASTWARD from Tomsk the Trans-Siberian Railway passes through a country of mountainous aspect. The foothills between the Obi River and Tomsk itself develop into mountain ranges, up which the road-bed of the railway is taken by many tortuous windings to the very top. As an engineering feat, the railway engineers have to be commended for the enterprise as a whole, but the shocking manner in which the line itself is laid will always preclude any decent pace being attained on its metals. Instead of cuttings or tunnelings, the whole line from Tigre to Krasnoiarsk is but a series of sharp curves. Rather than tunnel or cut through a bluff of insignificant proportions, the banking will be carried around in zigzag fashion, only to meet another bluff not a quarter of a mile away, which needs further curves.

Haste is shown in every feature of this section of the Siberian railroad. At the outset of the enterprise it was estimated that Irkutsk would be reached by the end of 1897; but while the laying of the road over the flat steppes from Chelabinsk to the Obi River offered no insuperable difficulties to the engineer, the mountains which had to be traversed further on had been looked upon with too optimistic an eye, and the consequence is that, in order to avoid borings or cuttings, the line has been carried many miles out of its way, at a cost far exceeding that which would have covered a properly laid and properly engineered road-bed.

I had conversations with several engineers on this subject, but I must confess that what I heard came rather as a shock to my ideas of Russian State enterprise. "You see," said one, "that we are engaged to lay this railroad. It is to be finished all the way in about three years' time; after that what are *we* going to do?" In other words, the suggestion was that it would be foolish to kill the goose which laid the golden eggs. And in corroboration of this I have heard many suggestions from influential people in Siberia that the construction of the railway has from its very commencement been one vast scheme of bribery, corruption, and general mismanagement. Accidents to the first trains to run over new sections have been numerous. On one new piece of road between Marinsk and Atchinsk the first engine to travel over the road disappeared bodily through the ballast into a small river below, necessitating a delay of several months for repairs and another excuse for extra pay. Still, all along that line there are signs of prosperity. The peasantry, heretofore employed in agricultural pursuits or the breeding of horses, are employed at wages which to them seem fabulous. Prices have gone up all round, and everybody seems more or less independent—and cheeky at that. Short-sighted, perhaps, for in a few years, when the construction of the line shall be completed, they will have to go back to their old pursuits, with less chance of making those pursuits remunerative.

A day and a half after leaving Tomsk the train arrived at the banks of the Chulim River, rather a small stream when compared to the Obi, Tom, or Irtish, but still broad enough to make two of the River Thames at London Bridge. A novel experience awaited us here, and one which we had not bargained for. As on the Obi, the bridge was not finished—in fact, only a couple of spans had been completed. The Russian engineer, however, did not do here what he did at Kreveschokovo. Instead of landing us out of the train to take sledges across the river, he made use of Nature's bridge, and that was the ice itself. A quarter of a mile from the river the rails diverted from the main road, and continued down the slope, and so on across the ice to the Atchinsk side. The whole thing was so unexpected and so novel that each one of us four gasped in astonishment. How deep the river was we did not know; and whether the ice was thick enough to bear the several hundreds of tons of locomotive and fifteen heavy carriages was another problem. Anyway, we were all glad when, as the train drew slowly up on the bank of the river, the conductor came up and requested us to descend and walk to the other side—cheerfully remarking that if the train went through only he, his fellow-conductors, and the engine-drivers would be drowned. We descended. A cheerless waste of ice stretched before us; beyond, over the river, we could see the glint of the sun on the brazen dome of a church in Atchinsk, with the twilight gathering in its greyness behind. The half-finished bridge stood out on our right, gaunt and spidery, and nothing around us but the eternal white of the snow.

Out came the passengers, a nondescript and

heterogeneous crowd, smothered in furs, and all looking like gigantic bales of wool. Down the bank and out on to the ice of the river we went; moujiks jabbering, Chinovniks hustling through the crowd, and we, more interested than any, slowly progressing in order to see the effect the train would have in its passage across the ice. A whistle sounded, then another, and yet another. The engine snorted, puffed, snorted again, puffed three or four times and got up way slowly, drew to the shelving bank and laboriously descended on to the ice. There was a distinct crunch as it did so, and another crunch when the first car rolled on; but gradually the whole train descended, and, at a pace not exceeding five miles an hour, moved across the frozen surface. As it passed us we felt the ice quiver, and heard innumerable cracks, like the reports of pistols in the distance; but the train got across the centre safely, spurted when near the bank, climbed up, and was on *terra firma* again.

THE END OF THE RAILWAY 107

As a novel piece of railway engineering, I think the passage of the Chulim River deserves commendation. Naturally it was impossible to nail the ties to the ice, but the Russian engineer had obviated this difficulty by freezing them on, and kept them frozen on by continual douches of water which was brought in buckets from a hole in the ice. I do not know the exact weight of that train, but it must have been considerably heavier than an ordinary English train, inasmuch as the carriages are built on a much more solid plan than our own. What struck me more than anything was the indifference which all the passengers, except ourselves, displayed in the affair. The taciturnity and nonchalance of the Russian becomes almost exasperating at times. Here, in face of what was distinctly a novel piece of railway travelling, there was no one with the exception of our four selves to pass a word of commendation, condemnation, or admiration of the feat.

Five minutes later we rolled into Atchinsk,

where three mortal hours were spent in a station which was, metaphorically speaking, little larger than a bandbox, and not half so comfortable.

Through the night on we went, toiling over mountain passes, through deep glens, or in and out gigantic forest glades, but with that eternal snow everywhere, with nothing around us which was inspiring or inspiriting. No moon, but with glinting stars that shed a pale light down upon a melancholy and deserted country. Morning broke, still we clattered on, but thankful that we were nearing our journey's end. In a few hours we should reach Krasnoiarsk, and there the Trans-Siberian Railway would end, and we should have to resort to the primitive method of locomotion which Siberians have known for hundreds of years, and which they still cling fondly to—the tarantass sledge.

In the early morning we were descending the slopes of the mountain range towards the valley of the Yenesei. Our train, in spite of the indifferently laid road, got up something like a speed at times, although I must admit the effect was not one to inspire confidence. Round narrow curves and over trestle bridges, high embankments, and across deep, sullen gorges, down which latter the very snow looked black and forbidding. It was a great time, then, when the conductor came and intimated that in one hour we should arrive at our journey's end. We commenced packing our traps with feverish haste; unpacked them again when we found that we wanted something; packed them up, and unpacked, in a delightful mood, engendered by the thoughts of something fresh in store. At length we descended into the valley of the Yenesei, and soon observed, from the end windows of the corridor carriages, the little white town of Krasnoiarsk away in the distance.

At the station we repeated our experience of Tomsk—with one stupefying alteration. This was the presentation of a hotel card by a dirty looking individual who said, in broken German, that he was an interpreter. Could it be possible that here, right out in the wilds of Siberia, we had struck some sort of civilization? An interpreter! We questioned him eagerly. What sort of hotel was it that he owed allegiance to?—meanwhile that clamorous drosky drivers, crowding around us, expatiated at length upon the merits of their particular horses.

More sledging and more bumping over the frost-bound roads. The station, as in duty bound, was three miles from the town, and a brisk drive of half an hour landed us into its main street.

I must confess, however, that my impressions upon arrival were considerably better than they had been on landing at Tomsk. Krasnoiarsk is smaller, but it is much cleaner, and its situation is one which cannot fail to elicit admiration. The tall mountains rear up all around it, and in the narrow cleft on a low belt of land, past which the broad and majestic Yenesei has its course, Krasnoiarsk lies. With the exception of the one opening in the cliffs the town is entirely sheltered; thus it was not surprising to find the snow not nearly so deep as we had found it in other parts of Siberia— in fact, on several parts of the high street we found our sledges running on the brown earth of the roadway—while the atmosphere was distinctly warmer than we had experienced so far.

The hotel which we put up at was attached to the post-station, a long low building, but surprisingly clean and well ordered in comparison with other Siberian hotels which we had stayed at. We even found, when on a voyage of discovery, a billiard-table in the basement, and great was our amazement thereat. The proprietor of the hotel, who was a Jew of the most Hebrew cast of countenance possible to conceive, busied himself to a great extent. He got us food in an incredibly short space of time, he did all that he could to assist us in our difficulties, and he did something more—and that was to ingratiate himself into our favour of his race.

It is freely stated that Krasnoiarsk will become in the space of a few short years the most important city in all Siberia. At the present time it is, like Tomsk, a town of merchants and gold-miners. It is something more—it is a penal settlement. About eighty per cent. of the population of Krasnoiarsk consists of exiles, and these include not only the very lowest class of the peasantry, but some of the wealthiest and most influential men of the town. In Siberia it holds something of a black name on account of its enormous percentage of exiled criminals, and I have heard it said that, so great is the bond between exile and exile, that the inhabitant who is a native-born Siberian, and not the descendant of a convict, is not only tabooed from the so-called society of the town, but has a very bad time in commercial matters. I give the following story for what it is worth, but it is related that a certain merchant of Krasnoiarsk found such difficulty in doing business with the inhabitants, in view of that bond of sympathy

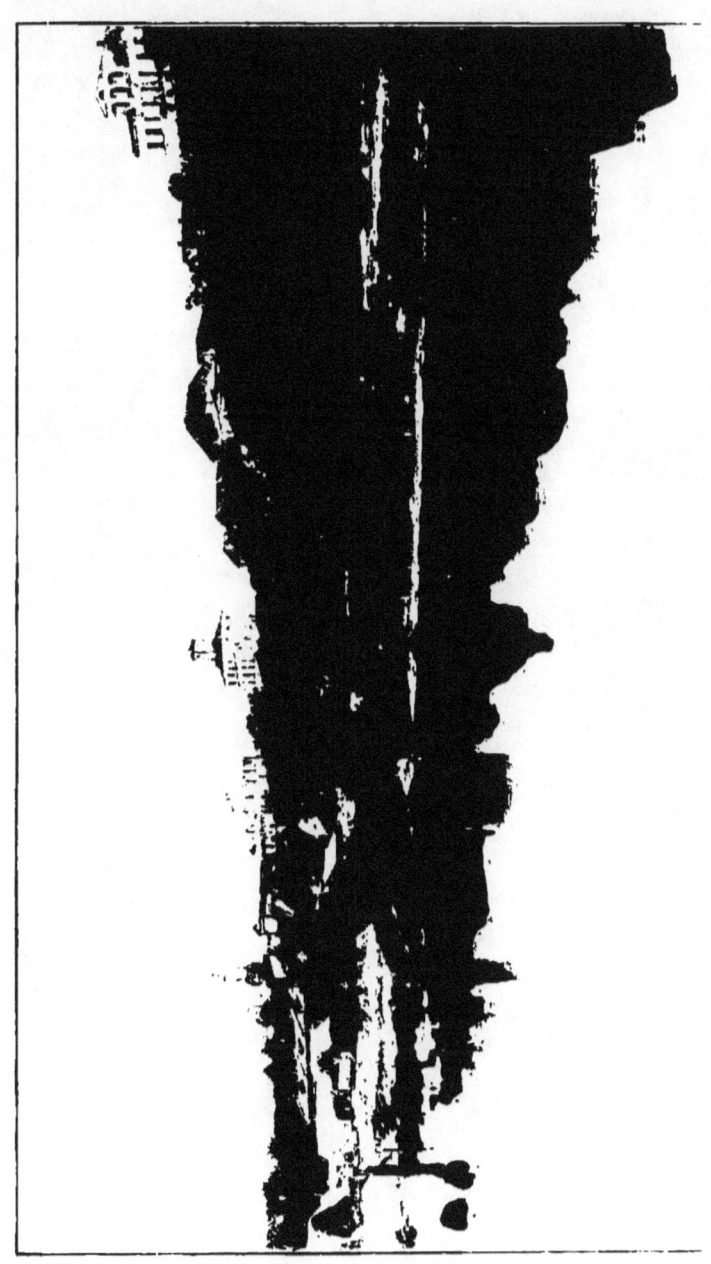

THE END OF THE RAILWAY 113

existing between the exiles, that he determined to become one of their class. To this end he journeyed to St. Petersburg, committed a crime, and was sent to Siberia in chains. After doing a short term of imprisonment in the Alexandrovsk prison at Irkutsk, he journeyed back to Krasnoiarsk, recommenced his business, and got on famously. Lie or no lie, I saw enough in my little stay in this penal settlement to convince me that, however little honour there may be amongst thieves, there is a great deal of sympathy.

To Englishmen Krasnoiarsk will be interesting from the fact that it is the point of debarkation for English steamers. A few years ago Captain Wiggins, an explorer of Northern seas, conceived the idea of forcing the passage of the Kara Sea to the mouth of the Yenesei River, and then to proceed by stream over a thousand miles to Krasnoiarsk. After many fruitless attempts he succeeded in his object, and to his success was due the formation of the Siberian Trading Syndicate.

I

The Russian Government was approached, and in order to encourage foreign enterprise in Siberia a special concession was given to the English syndicate, which allowed them to carry goods viâ the Kara Sea and the Yenesei River into the heart of Siberia, free of duty. At the time, it was predicted that nothing could stop the gigantic success of the enterprise, but bungling at home and an ignorance of the requirements of the Siberian trader led to complications and vicissitudes. Goods were sent out which were of no earthly use to the Siberians. Ships came along loaded to the very decks with goods which are to this day lying rotting or rusting on the banks of the Yenesei. Much money was lost, but considerable experience gained. The company was reconstructed again and again; but, hard on the heels of the enterprise, came the Trans-Siberian Railway, and whatever chances the Kara Sea route to Siberia may have had in the past, it is difficult to reconcile its success in the future with the construction of railway communication from the Baltic to the Pacific.

In this Siberian enterprise the name of Mr. Leyland Popham, a well-known London financier, stands out prominently. He has spent many thousands of pounds in the development of his hobby, and it is to be regretted that with special and unheard of concessions to foreigners in Siberia his enterprise should not have borne better fruit. It only exemplifies, however, the difficulty which all foreigners must experience in trading with a country so different in every respect to Europe.

The conditions of Siberia, it should always be remembered, are diametrically opposed to those of the Western states; but it is a difficult matter to convince the stay-at-homes of this fact, that they are not dealing with a civilized country, but one which is even more barbarous and primitive than the most barbarous and primitive of the British colonies. It is a country where prejudice ranks above everything, and where it is almost impossible to convince. The Siberian is not the sort of man who will accept for gospel truth, by means of an advertisement, that such and such a pick, or such and such a machine, are better than the implements which his grandfather used. What he wants you to do is to go there, demonstrate by actual working that your instrument *is* better than his, and then he will buy. This feeling has contributed more to the failure of foreign enterprise in Russia than many people are prone to admit.

Krasnoiarsk is also famous in connection with the Chinese tea trade. The tea traffic of Russia, as my readers are perhaps aware, is one of enormous proportions, and the Chinese tea which travels overland from the fertile valleys south of the Great Wall, over the Gobi Desert, through Urga, Kiakta, and Irkutsk, is handled in its commercial sense by the great tea-merchants of Krasnoiarsk. Most of this traffic occurs during the winter, when the frozen roads offer greater facilities for travel than during summer, when mud, sand, and deep dust makes travelling on the post-roads an extremely difficult undertaking. From the time when the snow fairly settles on the high-road, some time in October, until the break up in April, the whole road over the desert south of Lake Baikal, and the Yeneseik Mountains, is one line of tea caravans. It is sent in its original bales by the Chinese grower, but in Krasnoiarsk is redistributed to the various centres of the Empire. Many men have made fortunes out of the tea trade, which soon became almost a monopoly, and how this came about forms the subject of an interesting story.

Some forty years ago a certain merchant in Krasnoiarsk, who handled an enormous amount of Chinese tea, conceived the rather novel idea, at least to Siberians, of insuring his caravans. This was in the time when escaped prisoners, brigands, cut-throats, and general desperadoes thronged the high-road between Irkutsk and Krasnoiarsk, and as the caravans, each one consisting of some forty to fifty sledges, were in the charge of only two men to each caravan, there was considerable danger of not only losing the tea but also the horses. Our wily tea-trader, however, went even one better than the insurance scheme could give him. He actually employed thieves to stop his own caravans and steal his own tea. The stolen tea the hired thieves brought along to him by a circuitous route, and was sold by him *sub rosâ*, while he pocketed the insurance indemnity which the then guileless companies paid up with a liberal hand. By such methods as these, this particular tea-trader grew up in affluence, and, being in a land where swindling was only part and parcel of the general condition of things, when the bubble burst things were hushed up, and he went on his career smilingly, a rich man and an independent. Being an exile, however, and forbidden to leave Siberia for life, his wealth availed him little, for it could not be spent beyond the confines of his home. Still, the exercise of his capital was so great that in the few years of his trading he had been able to crush all formidable opposition, and could not only supply all markets of Siberia and European Russia at a cheaper rate than any other trader, but he was able to purchase from the Chinese grower a class of tea which could not be rivalled. Whether the Government was reluctant to make a scandal of his peccadilloes, or preferred to let things slide in consideration of the excellent tea with which this trader supplied the community it is difficult to say, but it only constitutes one of those peculiarities of Russian customs which are for ever offering problems to he who cares to think.

CHAPTER IX.

KRASNOIARSK.

WE had now arrived at the terminus of the Trans-Siberian Railway—the terminus so far as the early spring of 1897 was concerned. The road, we understood, would be completed as far as Kansk by May, to Nijniudinsk by the autumn, and to Irkutsk, the capital of Siberia, by the spring of 1898. Our journey from Krasnoiarsk was due south, towards the Syansk Mountains, and in order to cover the eight hundred odd miles which separated us from our goal, we had perforce to fall back upon the original Siberian method of locomotion, the troika sledge.

Pausing here, as we did, for several days, in order to complete our arrangements for that long and tedious journey, it may not be out of place to present a few facts with regard to the construction of the great Siberian railroad, an enterprise which is bound in future years to become a very important factor in the commerce of Asia. There are many political writers who assert that the great scheme covering the idea of a railway across Siberia was one of strategy. Considering the wealth of her Asiatic provinces, the Pacific littoral, and the Chinese border, and which have ever been poorly protected, and in the hope of bringing her Asiatic possessions into closer touch with Europe, Russia had looked at the matter in a calm and far-seeing light. Russians themselves, however, argue otherwise. They say that the main idea which dominated the scheme was commercial enterprise. For very many years, while Siberia has been growing in richness, and has supplied the mother-country with most of its commercial products, that country has been, even to Russians themselves, a land of mystery. It was the late Emperor Alexander's idea to construct the line—he was an imperialist if ever one sat upon the throne of Russia. His predecessors, however, if they had not shamefully neglected their Asiatic possessions, had at least treated them with indifference. Siberia has supplied for many years the finest furs to Moscow and St. Petersburg, the imperial coffers have been loaded with Siberian gold, and the finest stones have been sent from Siberia to Russia. There was the great Chinese tea trade passing through its heart, there was a demand all over that vast country for European goods, and yet there was no better means of sending them, or of bringing goods from Siberia itself, than by way of cumbersome and completely out-of-date caravans such as had toiled across those plains back in the dark ages.

The scheme of the Siberian railroad was one which recent political movements have had the effect of altering considerably. Starting from Chelabinsk, the line goes straight across the Tartar and Barabinski steppes, through the towns of Kurgan, Petropavlovsk, Omsk, Kainsk, to Kreveschokovo, crossing the important rivers of the Tobol, Ishim, and Irtish on its road. This section of the line is no less than 1320 versts long. I have already alluded to the reason why the railway, instead of describing a northerly course and taking in the town of Tomsk, went straight ahead to Atchinsk and Krasnoiarsk. After crossing the Obi, the line is continued to Atchinsk, 551 versts further on, crossing the rivers Tom and Chulim; then to Krasnoiarsk, another 169 versts; and after that Irkutsk, 1005 versts from the last-named town. So far, and in spite of the rather mountainous country between the Obi River and Lake Baikal, the laying of the line, it was considered, would not offer many difficulties to the engineer. The further project is to continue the line round the southern shore of the Baikal as far as Mysofsk, but here it is estimated tremendous difficulties will have to be encountered, for the line is to pass along a valley which is frequently inundated, and will necessitate the building of huge embankments. The valley of the Irkut is to be followed as far as the slopes of the Sirkisinsk Mountains, where it is to pass through the first tunnel constructed. In fact, the whole of that portion of the line running around the Baikal offers tremendous difficulties to the engineer—marshy grounds, hard rock, and numerous rushing streams having to be encountered. From here the line, according to the original plan, was to follow the course of the Selenga, which river it was to cross on a trestle bridge. Thence through a country of extreme mountainous character, including the Yablonoi chain, to the watershed of the Lena and Amoor, the course of the railway was one which only the most scientific railway engineers in the world would care to tackle. Nearing Stretinsk the line would be close to the Chinese border, which it was to follow closely, by the banks of the Amoor and the Ussuri, until it emerged from the mountains on to the coast and terminated at Vladivostock.

The railway was commenced at both ends, and the Vladivostock station was the first to be completed. A glance at the map will show that from Vladivostock the railway had to take an extreme northward course, in order to follow the Manchurian border, and at the time many of those interested in the enterprise looked longingly at that portion of Manchuria which alone obstructed a straight run across a flat and easily engineered country from Stretinsk to the coast. The Chino-Japanese War, and the political complications with Russia which occurred afterwards, came, for the latter country at any rate, at a most opportune time, and the result now is that the railway, instead of going to Vladivostock, as was the original intention, will now depart from the course at first laid down, and will cut into Manchuria and drive a straight course down to the Pacific coast at Port Arthur.

The save which will be effected in this later development of the Trans-Siberian Railway plan can only be appreciated when it is said that the original line from Stretinsk to Vladivostock would offer almost precisely similar difficulties to the engineer as those which the constructors of the Union Pacific Railroad met with, and that the new project involves nothing more terrible than laying the line on what is practically a hard, sandy desert. On top of this political stratagem comes the important fact that by cutting right into the heart of Chinese tributary states the Trans-Siberian Railway must and will absorb the bulk of the Chinese tea trade. As an instance of what this tea trade really means, it is as well to mention that while the greater portion of it heretofore has been carried by camel caravan across the Gobi Desert and through the heart of Siberia to Russia, enterprising traders have found that even a cheaper way to get tea into Russia has been to ship at Shanghai, and then by the Colombo, Suez, and Mediterranean route into the English Channel, trans-ship from here into the steamers for the Arctic seas, and thence by the Kara Sea route down into the centre of Siberia through the Yenesei River to Krasnoiarsk.

From end to end the line will be about seven thousand versts—4666 miles—but the construction of the main line itself does not complete the whole enterprise, which will be further increased by the development of the river traffic, in order to bring towns far inland in direct steamboat communication with the railway. Wharves and quays are to be built, branch lines sent out, and, in fact, as time progresses, the whole scheme is one ambitious enough to bring all the most important towns in Siberia into direct railway communication with the Western world. Of the colonization value of the railway I have already spoken. Siberia as a country is far richer agriculturally, and in many other respects, than is European

Russia, and although it will take time to convince the somewhat slothful Russian that Siberia is not all so black as it has been painted, the outlook is one decidedly of promise. As an earnest of the Government's endeavours to popularize this land so little known, foreign traders and travellers are offered privileges which one would scarcely dream of in connection with a country which heretofore has seemed unapproachable. For travellers, as a matter of fact, the Siberian Railway will offer many advantages. The zone system of railway travelling, which originated in Hungary, is in force throughout Russia, and at the present time it is possible to buy a first-class railway ticket at the port of Riga, on the Baltic coast, to Krasnoiarsk, right in the centre of Siberia, for the sum of £5 15s. This price is in such violent contrast to the excessive charges for horses under the older system of Siberian travelling that it surely cannot fail to have a very great effect upon the passenger traffic of Siberia in future years.

Having now done with the railway, we four exiles had perforce to turn our attention and our thoughts towards horses and sledges. The first thing to do was to buy sledges, and the next to hire horses. We had been told that, owing to the competition offered by the railway, we should find sledges cheap, especially in Krasnoiarsk. A decent sledge, new, will cost anything from two hundred to three hundred roubles; but this was not anything like the price which we intended to pay.

Realizing the fact that we were foreigners, with but a scanty knowledge of Russian, we were prepared to be fleeced a bit; but thanks to the good offices of our Jewish landlord, we got through the ordeal of sledge-buying to our complete satisfaction. The landlord knew a man who had a sledge to sell. I saw his little eyes twinkle with cupidity when we broached the subject of sledge-buying to him. He asked how much we were prepared to spend on the sledges. I casually mentioned twenty-five roubles. He raised his hands in horror.

K

Twenty-five roubles! Why, that would not purchase the runners! But we had a scheme which brought him to the business-like point, and that was to offer him a commission on the purchase, provided we were present, so that he should have no chance of making any ulterior arrangement with the seller. We arranged the commission on a sliding scale, so based that for every rouble he saved us so many more kopecks commission for him. Being shrewd, he saw the force of our argument, and I must say that in the subsequent proceedings he behaved as honestly as we could desire.

We drove down to his friend, where, under a shed, the sledge for sale was frozen hard and fast to the ground. We called forth the proprietor and demanded its price.

"A hundred roubles."

Our Jewish friend spat vigorously on the ground, called the other a moujik and a thief and several other hard names.

"A hundred roubles! Preposterous!" The foreigners would not dream of paying more.

than ten. There were plenty of other sledges in the town : and, in fact, if he did not want to sell, why the Jew himself, in commiseration for the foreigners, would lend them his own sledges!

This brought the proprietor down to seventy-five roubles. More spitting and more ejaculations on the part of the Jew.

At a signal we all walked towards the gate and our drosky. The proprietor ambled after us.

"Fifty roubles, then," said he.

"Fifteen roubles!" said the Jew.

"It is the only sledge I have," cried the other, raising both his hands in mock supplication. "If you take it from me I shall have to walk, for I must go to Irkutsk next week. There, there, it is a lovely sledge. Look at the runners, sound and bright as on the day they were put in. The body of the sledge too, roomy and comfortable; two gentlemen can sleep here day and night, if they wish. Come now, forty-five roubles."

"Twenty roubles," cried the Jew, with his foot on the step of the drosky.

"Bah!" cried the other, "you would rob me. Go your way."

He slammed the gate at us, and we all made as if to get into the drosky. But the Jew, however, motioned to us to wait for a moment; and then the gate opened, and the hairy face of the sledge-proprietor appeared. "Forty roubles," he cried in a sort of half howl.

"Twenty-five," responded the Jew.

"Not a kopeck less," said the owner.

"Then drive on, isvostchik," commanded the Jew.

The isvostchik struck the horse with the end of his reins; but the gate of the moujik's hut opened, and out the sledge-proprietor dashed.

"Thirty-five roubles."

"Twenty-six."

"Bah! you would rob me; say thirty."

"Not a kopeck more than twenty-seven."

"Twenty-seven, very well; but I must have ten kopecks for vodki."

Out of the drosky we bundled again into the yard; inspected the sledge, paid twenty-seven roubles for it, and ten kopecks for vodki; found the first three men we could in the street, and gave them a few kopecks to run the sledge round to the hotel, and the bargain was completed.

Another sledge was purchased with precisely similar proceedings, but I must confess that the whole business, irrespective of the undoubted fact that our Jewish friend pocketed a good round sum on the deal, turned out much cheaper than we had expected.

The next thing was to purchase our store of provisions, which was to last something like seven days; for during our passage of the Yenesei River as far as Minusinsk, the villages would be few and far between, and even in these villages the traveller would fare badly if he wanted food. The main post-road to Minusinsk was from Atchinsk, but the river road, we had been told, was vastly preferable to the post-road, in spite of the discomfort which would be experienced in having to travel long distances between villages. Nor could we have the assistance of the Government post-horses, and should have to rely upon what horses we could hire along the route in order to forward our journey. Why we had been advised to take the river route I cannot tell. I can only say that as it turned out it was a hundred per cent. dearer, two days slower, and a hundred times more uncomfortable than if we had taken the regular post-road through Atchinsk. But this fact was not brought home to us until the return journey was made and the regular method of communication resorted to.

The packing of a sledge is a task which only the experienced Siberian traveller should undertake. The body of the vehicle almost touches the ground, and it is in the body that all the stores are placed; careful packing with hay and straw, canvas and rope, ensuring a certain amount of rigidity. The goods are packed as nearly level as possible, and on the top are thrown heaps of straw, then the pillows, rugs, and furs of the traveller, who, poor fellow, is compelled, owing to the general flatness of the vehicle, to assume, during the whole of his journey, a more or less recumbent attitude. At the first set off, and when, smothered in our furs, we laid down in our sledges, everything seemed very jolly and comfortable, and I am sure we all looked forward with much avidity to our long sledge ride. It was after two days of it, however, when, what with the packages shifting and our cramped positions, we began to feel that, wretched as had been the accommodation of the Siberian railroad trains, one could at least move about in them with some degree of freedom.

It was afternoon before we were prepared to start on the first stage of the journey. The nearest village was fifty versts away, and a Krasnoiarsk moujik had guaranteed to take us there for the sum of eight roubles per sledge. Hours after the time appointed, he turned up with his six horses, a douga with its jangling bells hanging over each shoulder, a bottle of vodki under his arm, and a wooden pipe tucked between his teeth. Night was already falling, and we were anxious to be off, as we had no desire to have the first stage of our sledging accomplished in the dark. The leisurely manner in which this particular yemshik went about his business exasperated us, and it was already dark before we were able to scramble in, tuck ourselves in our furs, shake hands with the hotel proprietor, and give the signal to start.

And the start was made. The yemshik cracked his knout, gave vent to a piercing scream, followed it up by a whoop, and then the horses dashed forward as if they were pursued by demons. We went out of the yard of the hotel in a sort of a side slide, which brought us up against a wooden lamp-post on the opposite side of the road with a tremendous

THE YENESEI RAPIDS—SUMMER. [*To face page* 136.

jerk. Then down the road we careered; helter-skelter, bells jangling, and yemshiks shouting. Round a turn, under a wooden archway, erected to commemorate the visit of the Czarevitch; and then, with a plunge and a vision of flying snow from horses' feet, a cloud of steam from horses' nostrils, and with a sort of hold-on-or-be-thrown-out feeling permeating us, we went down the slope of the river-bank, out upon the glassy ice, with the whole broad expanse of the frozen Yenesei before us.

CHAPTER X.

DOWN THE YENESEI.

Night had already come on, but away behind us we could see the few pale lemon-coloured rays betokening the departure of the sun to other climes. Before us the river stretched, a great white mass with a low horizon and a mist beyond. We had got into a narrow cleft of the roadway, which zig-zagged in and out of gaunt pieces of ice, still and ghostly in the gloom.

Like the surface of the Obi, that of the Yenesei was all broken, jagged, and ragged, and the wonder was to me, as we passed swiftly over the bed of snow which concealed the ice beneath, how, in the first instance, the Siberian yemshiks had been able to make a passage over such a tumbled surface. The roadway was extremely rough, and we had not long been travelling before we began to feel how uneven was our bed, and how sharp were the corners of the boxes and bundles which made that up, comfortable indeed as it had seemed at the moment of setting out.

But there was a solemnity about it all which could not fail to make the experience one to inspire thought. The front of the sledge was open, but, in spite of the still air which reigned around, the speed of the horses caused a draught which sent quite a cutting wind in our faces, to leave congealations of frost on eyebrows, eyelashes, and beards. Wrapped up almost to our eyes in furs, and with such an amount of rugs on top of us that it was quite impossible to move, we did not, at least for the first hour or so, feel the cold. But how cold it was one could realize when looking out, with blinking eyes, at the expanse beyond; or, closer in, to the yemshik, whose burly figure was limned against the white and yet whose clothing was covered with hairs of frost; or upon the horses at the side, whose backs and whose legs were white. Beyond the jangle of those douga bells, beyond the crack of the yemshik's knout, beyond the occasional wailing cry which he gave vent to in order to encourage his willing steeds, or beyond the crunch of the runners on the snow, or the patter of the hoofs when the snow was left for some expanse of bare ice, there was no sound to be heard. Dimly to the right and the left we could see the banks of the river, simply mounds rising above the surface. And thus on we went; the horses ever at a gallop, the yemshik sitting on one side of the sledge, feet dangling almost beneath the runners, whip trailing idly in the snow, head bowed, and face smothered in his sheepskin pelisse. Nothing to break the monotony of it all, unless it were sleep. Behind us every now and again, when some turn in the roadway brought us round, we could hear the tinkle of the bells of our companions' troika.

Occasionally, as if only to break the awful solitude which seemed to fill the very air, one or the other of us would shout, and shout back; occasions which called forth no resentment on the part of the yemshik, in spite of the fact that every shout made the horses go faster.

What a ride that was! My companion Gaskell sought slumber; but I, filled with the mood of reflection, could only sit and gaze upon—what? the nothingness around me! To listen to the musical clanging of the bells, to the hoof-beats of the horses, and to wonder what in the name of Heaven the yemshik was talking about.

For he had a peculiar way, this yemshik. The little I could catch of his talk referred to doves and pigs. He would address the starboard horse in the most affectionate terms, and a second later would bring his long knout with a swishing crack above the head of the beast to port, and hurl terrible invectives at it, meanwhile that the equine representative in the centre went along with great swinging strides, loaded down, as it seemed, with the great douga, and undoubtedly deafened with the noise of the bells around his ears.

Minutes went into hours, but there was no cessation in the pace; there was no alteration in the surroundings, unless it was that with the advent of the stars things became clearer and more distinct. Thus I could see on either side the greenish blue ice which stood up like points of rock all around us, and I could more distinctly perceive the rugged banks of the river which now began to tower on either side. Once, when we had travelled some two hours out of Krasnoiarsk, we burst suddenly on a plain of ice uncovered by snow, and over whose clear surface the horses scrambled at a mad pace, and the runners swished as a fast steamer would through water. Passing over such a surface as this could be compared to nothing so much as riding in a boat, for the ice beneath was black, and glittered like still water. But we were soon over that expanse, swept clean as it had been by blustering winds, and in among the hummocky ice again, on the bed of snow; ever tearing onward, the yemshik ever talking, the whip occasionally cracking, a periodical shout from our comrades, a far-off tinkle of the bells of their sledge, and the more clamorous tones of our own.

Three hours of this, and I saw the driver making a bee-line for the bank. As he approached nearer and nearer, he urged his horses to faster pace, stood up on the seat, shouted and gesticulated as a madman would; while his little horses tugged and strained at the traces, galloping like fury all the time, clouds of steam pouring from their nostrils and rising above their heads, and with every hair upon their bodies coated with white ice. The bank was reached, a short sharp clatter over the bare ice by the side, and then up the slope at a swinging pace, round the corner, and, almost before I knew it, we had passed a house, another, and then another, all black and sombre in this darkness. One more corner, and we swung into a street; not a light to be seen, not a sign of life; still on at that wild gallop, until, with a jerk and a huge side-slip, we pulled up before a small hut, which, to say the least, looked anything but hospitable.

"First station," cried the yemshik, as he laboriously descended from his seat and went round to pick the ice from the nostrils of his horses. "First station, barins. Please go in and have the samovar."

Out we bundled. The second troika had arrived, and out *they* bundled. We asked each other what we all thought about it, and the general verdict was one of approval. Novelty is a great thing, and while variety is the spice of life, how could any one grumble, spite of hard corners and that biting cold?

The moujik's hut which we were bidden to enter was graced with one of the smallest doorways I have ever seen. It was certainly not more than four feet high. There was much banging of heads in order to get through, more banging in ascending a short flight of wooden stairs which led us into a small corridor, unlighted, but smelling very badly. By diligent groping, one of us managed to find the handle of a door, which door, owing to the enormous amount of padding on its edges, persistently refused to open until two of us had exerted our strength upon it, although it was no bigger than the one which gave entrance to the passage.

A burst of light and a cloud of steam preceded our entrance. Bending low we entered the single room of the moujik, a room not more than six feet high, and which poor Scawell, who was tall enough to be a Lifeguardsman, found to be particularly inconvenient. It was a veritable moujik's apartment, and one which was so truly Russian that it deserves more than passing description.

As we entered, it was to perceive on one side a huge brick stove, which gave off a fierce heat, and upon the top of which the lord and master of the house reposed in slumber.

A bench, in no wise dissimilar to the tap-room benches of the English public-house, occupied another side. Depending from the ceiling upon the end of a long birch pole was a curious arrangement, which, upon closer inspection, turned out to be a cradle. This was simply a shallow wooden dish, supported at each end by string, terminating in a knot tied upon the end of a rope, which in turn was attached to the birch pole. Little curtains hung on the rope and surrounded the peacefully sleeping infant in the dish, the limber pole above giving this primitive cradle a gentle motion, highly calculated to soothe the slumber of the moujik's baby.

But the heat—pouf! it was terrible. Coming in as we had from that piercing cold right into a perfect hothouse, our beards and eyelashes thawed in a moment, and the water streamed down our faces. There was a smell of furs and skins, which did not improve the atmosphere. A little old woman was sleeping on the bench in one corner; a younger woman, in short red petticoat, a red shawl around her head, and a thin cotton blouse open at the front and exposing her whole bust, and with bare feet, had busied herself on our entry. Without signal or asking she had put some pieces of paper and sticks in the samovar and was engaged in lighting it.

Such is the way of the Siberian traveller. This was no post-station—it was simply a peasant's hut; but it was the custom of travellers to enter unannounced, uninvited, any house in a village and demand accommodation.

It was while consuming the contents of the samovar, and some food which we had brought with us, that our yemshik, who by some manner of means had got rid of the thick coating of ice which covered his features on our arrival, entered, and, after laboriously crossing himself before the small ikon in the corner of the hut, requested to know if it was the wish of their excellencies to proceed to the next stage that night, or to remain until day broke. Anxious to get on, we plumped for proceeding without delay; and the yemshik departed in his search for horses.

We now began to see the folly of not having taken the main post-road, for it was some three hours before six horses could be found in that village to take us on to the next stage; even then it was only by paying exorbitant prices, and after much harangue with half a dozen sturdy and extremely vociferous moujiks, who crowded heavily into the chamber, that we were able to get horses at all.

Looking back at that scene—that tiny, low-pitched room; my lord of the house slumbering comfortably on top of the stove; the bare floor; those walls constructed of unplaned tree-trunks; the tiny windows; the bench with its ornament of a steaming samovar; the swinging cradle, and the general primitiveness of everything—it is hard to realize it all occurred so short a time ago. The remembrance comes vivid of the patient, yet indescribable look of the woman, her wondering eyes at our, to her, incomprehensible tongue. But with the discomfort of it all worn off by the swift hand of time, one comes to almost appreciate its primeval originality.

We paid a few kopecks for the accommodation we had had. The yemshik received his roubles and a few kopecks besides, which is humorously called "tea money" in Siberia, although it is safe to say it is always spent in vodki. Then off we went again.

A fleeting vision of village huts; down the bank and out upon the river once more; a different yemshik, but with precisely similar methods and mannerisms as characterized our first. Another three hours of it, during which I tried to snatch a little sleep; only to be awakened at intervals when the runners of the sledge would strike some obstruction, and force the corner of some more than particularly hard box into my ribs. Well into the night the second stage was reached; more horses procured, then on we went again, obtaining spells of sleep of ten minutes to a quarter of an hour's duration, and thus we managed to get through the night. But, as the grey morning began to creep over the hilltops ahead of us, it was cold, weary, and sore that we were. In spite of our heavy clothing it had been an utter impossibility to keep out the cold, for it attacked us in all directions, and it was only by liberal doses of cognac that we seemed to manage to keep our circulation going at all.

It was a sublime sight to see the sun rise over the frosted peaks ahead, while the hummocky ice around assumed all the colours of the rainbow. As the sun's rays became stronger, they tinged in glowing colours the hillsides, which now reared themselves up from the very banks of the river. We could perceive great stalactites of ice depending from rocks, and which were, in summer, cascades. The huge pieces of ice which crowded in on all sides of us, forming the surface of the river, at times assumed enormous proportions and most grotesque designs. Sometimes they would tower right above, or would appear as mounds; piece piled upon piece until they looked like small pyramids. The banks, too, were heaped with these broken lumps, not one of them less than three to four feet in thickness. When the sun finally burst over the hilltops it was a magnificent spectacle which met our gaze down that wide river, all hemmed in as it was by beetling rocks. One could realize then what this river was in summer; a great rushing waterway, passing through scenery majestic in its grandeur, but now with its water held tight and immovable in the grasp of the ice king.

CHAPTER XI.

AN EXCITING ADVENTURE.

For two days and nights we travelled thus, and, as we progressed up the river towards the mountain ranges, the scenery around became extremely grand and wild, the banks occasionally crowding into a narrow gorge, with the cliff-sides of black slate and sandstone rearing themselves up in perpendicular walls for many hundreds of feet. Villages became few and far between, and more primitive, so that occasionally we were compelled to remain in some woodman's hut for hours at a stretch, awaiting as patiently as possible the arrival of fresh horses. Nor did the surface of the river road improve, for the traffic became less and the track frequently ran through virgin snow. Four days out of Krasnoiarsk the cliffs on either side of the river road subsided, and we passed into the steppe of Minusinsk. This steppe is one of the most peculiar in Siberia, situated as it is at the bottom of a circle of huge mountains, through which the Yenesei runs.

It was while traversing this region that we experienced a sensational incident which served considerably to break the monotony of the journey. At a small village, some one hundred miles north of Minusinsk, we had chartered six sorry-looking steeds to drag us on to the next stage. It was a case of taking them or nothing, and, to add to the difficulties of the situation, the yemshik who was to drive the first troika, containing Gaskell and myself, was hopelessly drunk at the start. The horses, it was clear, had been wretchedly kept, two of them being nothing but skin and bone; still, we had seen some wretched specimens of equine prowess so far, and did not pass much comment.

It was night when we started—a night so black that the darkness could almost be felt. The driver, maudling and hiccoughing, had been helped to his perch by some of the villagers, and we set off along the narrow roadway at the usual gallop, which, however, owing to the inferiority of the horses, soon dwindled down into a mere shuffle through the snow. We had gone to sleep, and it must have been some hours after our departure from the village when Gaskell awakened me and said he thought something was the matter.

Looking out through the tarpaulin of the sledge, we could see nothing but blackness around, with the exception of the thin light thrown up from the snow. The sledge was at a standstill, and our shouts to the yemshik brought forth no response.

Where were our companions?

I bundled out of the sledge, feeling at the same time so numbed that it was with difficulty I could move. I shouted when I got out, in the hope of attracting our companions; but no response came. I felt along the sledge, thinking that perhaps the driver, drunk, had gone to sleep and allowed his horses to wander, and as I went, sunk up to my knees in the deep fleecy snow.

The driver's perch was empty; and just then I stumbled over one of the horses, which was lying buried up to its neck in the snow. Gaskell joined me, and at once the full horror of our situation burst upon us. It was clear that the driver had fallen from his seat, and that the horses, left to themselves, had wandered off the track at their own sweet will.

We had in the sledge a bicycle lantern which had been brought with us from England. This we lit, and by its feeble light took in as much as we could of the situation. The runners of the sledge were completely buried in deep snow; the horses were likewise stuck fast; and a closer inspection showed one of them to be dead—literally frozen to death.

How were we to get out of the difficulty? Gaskell suggested shouting for our companions: but that was little use. The second troika had probably gone straight ahead on the track, and we had no means of knowing how far off it we were, and there was no telling how soon the other horses, sorry animals that they were, would survive the piercing cold and their inertion.

A glance at the watch showed us that it was three o'clock, and another five hours must elapse before dawn would appear. What to do was at first difficult to decide. To wander off in search of assistance was not to be thought of, as we had no means of telling in which direction the horses had wandered— whether to the north or the south bank of the river. We made a short circuit of the sledge, but nowhere could we find traces of ice. To go forward seemed impossible, and yet to remain as we were was equally risky. Food and drink we had with us, fortunately; but with no means of knowing where we were, it was impossible to tell how long it might be before we could get succour.

There was, however, just one way out of the difficulty, and that was to retrace on the marks made by the sledge runners, if that could be done with two horses. This was the plan decided upon. We cut the dead horse adrift, and, using some of the spare rope as whips, we stood on either side of the living, and lashed them until our arms ached. The poor beasts were nearly succumbing. They lay flat on their stomachs, nibbling at the snow, and our kicks and blows for a time seemed to have no more effect upon them than if they were made of wood. At length, however, we succeeded in getting them to move. We helped by pushing the sledge, and gradually got it round into the track. Then, step by step, with much floundering and many falls, we began to retrace our way. All this in a pitch darkness, in a raw cold that pierced us, and in momentary expectation of one or the other or both the horses dropping dead.

An hour of this sort of work brought us to the river-bank, and here we were so exhausted that we were compelled to rest a few moments, while the horses, with drooping heads and trembling frames, looked fit to fall. To have arrived at the river was at any rate something of a blessing, but how to get on the road again was another difficulty; for on the river surface we could trace no sign of the sledge runners, while the jagged pieces of ice which stuck up all around made forward progress look impossible. The only way out of it was for one of us to go across the river in order to discover the road.

This duty Gaskell took on. He carried the lantern with him, and I was to show the whereabouts of the sledge after his departure by signals with lighted matches. He disappeared into the darkness, but the occasional flash of his lantern as he crawled over the hummocks showed me in his direction. Across the river he went, the spark of light growing fainter and fainter as he progressed, ultimately disappearing altogether, and I was left alone in that vast solitude, in the middle of the night, with no sound but the heavy breathing of my two exhausted horses or the just faintly perceptible rumble of the river beneath the ice.

Five minutes, ten minutes passed, and then a shout was wafted to my waiting ears on the cold air. I shouted in reply, and saw the faint glint of Gaskell's light away in the distance. He was coming round by a circuitous route, and in a quarter of an hour rejoined me, with the welcome intelligence that by following the bank of the river for a short distance a gap in the hummocks led to the road.

The work it was to get those poor tired horses to start again! It was useless to show mercy, for it was clear that they could not last out much longer. Our compass told us which was the direction to follow, and once having gained the track we set off as hard as we could get the horses to go, both of us on the seat, alternately shouting and whipping.

What relief we both experienced when, around a bend in the river, we saw a sparkle of light away up on the left bank! I got out the bicycle lantern, lit it, and waved it in the air. Then on the faint breeze came the sound of a cry. Some one was evidently looking out for us, and we urged our horses to their topmost pace. Another shout, and yet another, and presently we distinguished the voices of Scawell and Asprey. Ten minutes later we struggled up the bank of the river almost into the arms of our comrades, who had been anxiously awaiting our arrival.

Judge of our astonishment when we learned that they had had an almost similar experience to our own. They had been travelling behind us, and not four versts out of the village from which we had started one of their side horses dropped dead, was cut away, and the journey resumed with the two remaining horses. But their sledge being heavy they could not travel at more than a walking pace, and their anxiety

can be imagined when, on arrival at the village, they found that we were absent and nothing had been heard of us. In this part of the country, where murder and robbery are of frequent occurrence, all sorts of surmises and conjectures may be aroused; but, safe out of the difficulty, we had no mood now but to give our first thoughts to the fate of the yemshik. It was obvious that the poor fellow must have dropped asleep and fallen off his box. Where and when it was impossible to say, and his fate seemed as good as sealed, for in that terrible cold, hardened Siberian though he might be, he could scarcely survive the inevitable.

One thing was remarkable, and that was the indifference which the villagers and his brother yemshik displayed regarding his fate. We were anxious to organize a search-party, but none of them evinced any great willingness to enter upon the expedition. He would be sure to turn up, they said; why bother? If he had liked to make a beast of himself and fall from his sledge, that was surely his look out! No self-respecting yemshik ought to do such a thing as that. Our arguments had little avail, and, I confess it with shame, none of us four felt called upon to undertake the task on our own responsibility, even if we had horses with which to perform the task.

Life is cheap in Siberia! We had already heard so much of men being frozen to death, of murders, and of general carelessness in regard to human life, that even we, I fancy, were growing somewhat callous, and we did what Nature called for first, and that was to sleep. We were awake with daylight, prepared to continue our travelling, when our inquiries regarding the fate of the yemshik revealed the fact that a couple of men had gone down the road in order to find him; and we were fain to leave the matter at that.

Fresh horses being engaged, we resumed our journey, and that night galloped into the town of Minusinsk, the last township north of the Chinese border. There was no inn or hotel at Minusinsk, but our yemshik had a friend whose practice it was to put up travellers for the night; so we drove immediately to the house, in order to obtain its shelter and comfort, however poor that might be. To our delight the house turned out to be superior, if anything, to the hotels which we had seen so far in Siberia. It was at least roomy and clean, and was kept by a Livland exile, who spoke German. We had the experience of a meal of cutlets and white bread, washed down with a flagon of red Caucasian wine. What matter if we did sleep on the bare boards, or that the only illumination we had was by means of candles which wanted perpetual snuffing! To what we had been accustomed during the past few days on the river, the exile's house in Minusinsk was a veritable palace. We slept, and slept soundly; awoke and had our samovar, more white bread, and some eggs. We made a tour of the town, our exit into the street being signalized by the appearance of a Chinaman on the opposite side removing the shutters of a tea-house. It was a glimpse of the Oriental which had a significance for us—a hint that we were close upon the borders of another land. Bad as were the Russian facias to decipher, they were easy compared to the numerous hieroglyphics in Chinese which we now occasionally stumbled across in our perambulations of Minusinsk.

There was not much to be seen in the town. It was a mere huddle of one-story frame-houses, with a rather fine church and a barracks—for Minusinsk was the depôt for the Cossacks used in the control of the Altai gold-mining system. There was a bank also, merely a hut in itself, but sufficient for our purposes, and here we changed some of our big paper money into small silver pieces, for south of Minusinsk we were to go into a country which was almost uninhabited.

As an illustration of the manner in which the Russian officials keep watch over all strangers in the vast dominions of the Czar, it was interesting to find that we had been expected. Our return from the ramble found the chief of police in our apartment, attended by a couple of Cossacks of most formidable dimensions. He knew all our names, knew where we had come from, and where we were going. He signed our passports; urbanely drank tea and vodki with us, shook hands on his departure, and wished us the best of luck.

An incident like this was very instructive as to the manner in which the eye of the law is fixed upon the foreigner in autocratic Russia.

CHAPTER XII.

NEARING THE CHINESE FRONTIER.

AT Minusinsk we were to leave the Yenesei, and continue our journey to the Syansk Mountains over the foothills, which now intervened between the Chinese border. Beyond one or two villages at decidedly long intervals, we could look forward to nothing in the shape of accommodation until we reached Karatuski, a village of rather larger dimensions than the majority, and which was the last Siberian habitation before the frontier. From Minusinsk to Karatuski, there was no semblance of a road, merely a track formed in the snow by the telegas of the gold-miners going to or returning from the mines. Southward from Minusinsk the whole country was gold-bearing, and Karatuski itself was the head-quarters of the goldmasters during the summer operations.

After a day's rest in Minusinsk we once more resumed our journey, our way being over the barren uplands which were ever rising towards the mountain range. Very little incident marked our progress during the first day's journey, and on the second we came in sight of the ragged spurs of the mountains which mark the Chinese frontier. At midday on that day we had reached, after a long toilsome drag up-hill, the top of one of the foothills, and the scene round us was one truly magnificent. To the north the whole snow-covered country lay stretched like a panorama. To the south tumbled hills dwindled away in the distance, and, then, above them, with peaks glittering and glinting in the sunlight, rose the cones of the Altai range. To the east more mountains, all peaked, shaggy, and uneven. They were hills and mountains such as are seen in no part of the world except Asia. There were no bluffs or rounded domes, but sheer heaps of rocks pointing up to the sky like reversed stalactites.

On the evening of the third day we passed through a narrow gorge on the ice of a small river, and ultimately came to Karatuski. Here we were met by several Siberian gold-miners, who had been expecting our arrival, and who were, even so early in the year, making their preparations for the forthcoming season's work. Karatuski was but a village, still we had no difficulty in finding fairly comfortable quarters in a moujik's house, and as our stay in the village was to be of some days, during which we had to buy provisions and engage men for our expedition in the mountains, we made no bones about engaging two houses in which to get as much comfort as it was possible during the time.

On the very day of our arrival, and while we were doing full justice to our first meal, we were besieged by quite a crowd of peasants who came to be engaged. Somehow the

MINUSINSK. [*To face page* 168.

rumour had gone forth that foreigners were coming into the country, and would require labourers. Whether the peasants thought that they were likely to get better pay or better treatment from the foreigners, I do not know, but anyway they came in their hundreds, and not even our oft-repeated refusals to have anything to do with them until next day would rid us of them. Some assured us that they had walked forty or fifty versts from neighbouring mines on the chance of being engaged, and one interesting party, consisting of nearly two dozen Livlanders, who all spoke German, and were all convicts, begged and prayed of us to engage them. Our interview with some of these worthies threw some sidelights upon Siberian goldmining, for ninety per cent. of the workers at the mines, it appeared, were of the criminal class.

At Tomsk we had been very careful to make inquiries as to the class of workmen to be obtained in the Minusinsk district, and had been assured that no criminals were sent to the gold-mining districts. The contrary we found was the case, for out of over two hundred men who presented themselves to us not one per cent. bore the passport of a free man; but had, instead, the police certificate which detailed the crime and the sentence of the holder. It is interesting to record that we engaged six men, the most likely-looking and the most intelligent of the mob, and that each one of them had been banished for life to Siberia for no less a crime than violent murder. The most intelligent of the lot was a German Livlander, name, August Schultz, who had committed two murders, one in Courland and one in Siberia, and enjoyed a wife who had distinguished herself by beating out the brains of a former husband with a hatchet. We engaged Schultz as our interpreter, and his wife as our cook, although mentally resolving at the time that it would be necessary to keep a loose eye on the doings of our employés.

When one of the gold-masters came to assist us in getting the police permission for these men to travel with us, his horror at the discovery of the sort of people we had engaged was something most interesting to witness.

"If you had searched all Siberia," said he, "you could not have found six worse desperadoes than those you have got. Why did you not come to me and let me get you different men?"

"But they are the most likely-looking of the lot who came for engagement!"

"That I agree; I have had one or two of them working for me, and they have been amongst the best, until they broke loose and started fighting. These men, realizing that they have to remain in Siberia, and always as the meanest of workmen, care nothing for their lives; but you are responsible for them, and if one kills the other you will have to pay the bill. However, I wish you the best of luck."

As events turned out, we had nothing to

complain of with regard to our men. We paid them liberally, and they appreciated the fact, and it was a spectacle to behold when, after giving them hand-money for their engagement, they simultaneously flopped down on their knees and severally kissed our boots. According to them we were all "excellencies," and they paraded the little village to the envy and chagrin of the rest of the crowd who had come on the chance of being engaged.

Our first duty was to proceed to a gold-mine some three or four versts north of the frontier. Our papers, brought from Moscow, duly *viséd* and passed in Tomsk, had to be laid before the local mining inspector at Karatuski, and it was then that we began to realize what red-tapeism in Russia means. I had already received from the Minister of Mines a personal concession which gave me the right to explore for gold in the whole of Siberia, either to rent or buy existing mines or to prospect for new ground. Our object in first of all looking over a mine already in existence was to get an idea of the manner in which the Siberian works for the precious metal. Two of us were experts from Western Australian and South African gold-fields, and one of us had practical experience of Siberian mining on the Amoor River. From Western Australia and South Africa to the Syansk Mountains is a far cry, and customs and methods were naturally expected to be very diverse. Having deposited our papers, it was my pleasant duty to sign a formidable-looking document which bound me responsible for the lives of the seven human beings in our employ. I then signed another paper guaranteeing that I would not sink a shaft more than so many feet deep, that I would never allow any brawling or strikes, that I would not encroach upon another man's land, that I would faithfully keep a record of every particle of gold from wheresoever obtained while prospecting, and a dozen or more similar documents which tied our little party hand and foot to the Government, each document having to be stamped, sealed, tied up with red tape, signed by half a dozen functionaries, and so on, until we all became heartily sick of the whole proceedings. They gave us a gold-book in which was to be entered most accurately every piece of gold obtained, how much earth was dug out in order to obtain it, its weight, nature, and consistency. I must admit, however, that while all these rules and regulations looked bewildering in their formidability, the Russians did their very best to impress upon us the necessity of following them to the letter.

While in Karatuski, it may not be out of place to give a little idea of how some of the rich Siberian gold-miners spend their time during their self-imposed exile in this bleak and inhospitable region. Karatuski is simply a village, and the dwellings composing it, although at least a dozen of them are owned by rich miners, are nothing more than mere log houses. In honour of our visit we received many invitations to parties and to dinners, and here the ludicrousness of Siberian customs came once more very much to the fore. Imagine a log house in a village of less than a thousand inhabitants. Imagine a room the walls of which are composed of beams laid one on the other, the floor bare boards, a rough table in the centre, and scarcely any more ornamentation. Imagine, on top of this, a dinner-party given in the middle of the day and everybody in evening dress! The stiffness and formality were really embarrassing at times. Most of the miners, rich men though they were, were of the commonest type of Russians, uncultured either in manners or education. Their very riches seemed to press upon them like a load. They had some idea that it was necessary to be hospitable, but they had not the experience or the knowledge which would tell them how to go about it.

On several of our visits I noticed many side-glances of suspicion, as to whether or not we were criticizing them. Their intentions were good; they did the best they could for us according to their light, and we appreciated that sentiment above everything. It was impossible, however, not to realize how farcical the whole thing was. There was nothing homely about it, nothing that would tend to make a man feel as a guest should amongst friends; and, above all, it was impossible for us to talk much with them, on account of our limited knowledge of the language. Neither could we enter upon the drinking bouts which were so frequent; nor take part in those solemn card-parties which extended far into the night.

For the Siberian there is but little excitement or amusement than that afforded by cards. In every house that we went to in Karatuski, at least those possessed by the miners, there were the inevitable card-tables, their solemn-faced ring of players, the heaps of paper money at each man's elbow, the eternal shuffle and click of the cards. High stakes are the rule. Gold-mining in any country can hardly be set down as a commercial enterprise, and in Siberia least of all. Men who were peasants a few years

KARATUSKI.

To face page 176.

ago find themselves millionaires to-day, are overwhelmed by their wealth, and in cards seek a relaxation from the monotony of their lives. I have it on good authority that several of the richest men in Siberia have lost their whole fortune in one night's play, have started work again, and in a few years have made another only to be spent once more at the card-table. One of our hosts related quite frankly, and with a smile on his face, that in three nights he lost two hundred thousand roubles. Certainly one of the most peculiar aspects about it is that in the matter of playing it was the millionaire gold-miner who lost and invariably the Government functionary who won. It was common sight for us in our various visits to see the staff, mere clerks, of the mining inspectors, the honoured guests of the establishment. Most of these men receive from the Government not more than seventy-five roubles a month, but that little oval cockade in their caps and their shoulder straps which make them Chinovniks, have an awe-inspiring effect upon the average Russian. I have seen such clerks playing for stakes of a thousand roubles upwards, and a close observation has shown me how little they lose. One is apt to cogitate, then, on the possibility of a good proportion of the miners' losses not being quite unintentional.

In order to proceed to our destination, it was necessary to abandon our big sledges at Karatuski, and to take smaller sledges, each drawn by one horse, for the rest of the journey. These sledges, as well as the horses which were to take us to the mountains, had to be purchased. The former were merely tiny basket arrangements fixed on a couple of runners, and were about as ramshackle as one could possible conceive. The track over the mountains being an extremely narrow one, it would be quite impossible to take the larger and wider sledges. The purchase of fifteen horses and fifteen sledges, which were to form our caravan—one man to each sledge, and three sledges to contain our provisions—was naturally an expensive undertaking in such a place as Karatuski. I have no doubt that we were cheated right royally, but that could not be helped under the circumstances.

Our first day's journey was to be one of eighty versts along the course of the River Armcul, one of the tributaries of the Yenesei. At eighty versts from Karatuski, the miners of the district had erected a hut for the shelter of those making their way to and from the mines, and at every succeeding eighty versts a similar hut had been placed, these being all maintained by the miners, who contributed a certain amount per year for their maintenance.

On the morning of a day late in January, our preparations being all complete—the baggage-sledges packed, the men all together, the horses in their sledges, and everything ready for our two hundred miles' drive to the mine—we set out. Each man had to drive, but as the roadway was one cut through the deep snow, the question of getting off the road was not one to be concerned about, as right or left of the track the snow was ten to twelve feet deep, and impossible to get through. The whole population of the village turned out to see us off. There was much cracking of whips, shouting, and other to-do as the caravan moved slowly up the hill, rounded the corner, and in a few moments was out of sight of Karatuski, with nothing but the glaring white uplands ahead.

CHAPTER XIII.

IN THE SYANSK MOUNTAINS.

For some distance our way led over a few short hills to the banks of the Armeul, our progress being characterized from the very start by frequent upsets. I can only describe the roadway, if roadway it can be called, as one of the most villainous I had ever seen. The method of making it was indeed primitive, for instead of selecting a circuitous route, in order to avoid bad places, it went dead ahead, and in doing so, yawning gaps occurred, down which our sledges fell, almost on top of the horses, and with jerks and creakings which threatened to dismember every vehicle. The horses slithered down the slopes, struggled and squirmed up the other side, and could only be kept going at times by much whipping and fierce shouting.

Nearing the Armeul, we came out on the crest of a small hill which bordered the river, and here an amusing, although somewhat serious, incident befell our party. The runners of previous passing sledges had cut a deep groove in the snow, and so long as we kept in this groove all was well. Arrived on the slope, Gaskell's horse, infuriated at the frequent whippings he had received, plunged heavily sideways, the runners of the sledge got out of the groove, and in a second the whole lot—sledge, horse, and driver—went rolling down the snow in one confused heap towards the river. As chance would have it, the edge of the river was bare of ice, where the border had been broken away by water-carriers. Into this the horse fell with a tremendous splash, dragging with him the sledge, and sunk in about eight feet of water. For a time it was impossible for us to do anything to assist our companion, who, fortunately, had been thrown clear of the sledge, and was stuck fast up to his armpits in the soft snow. When we did reach him, it was gratifying to find that no bones were broken, and we quickly hauled him back on to the roadway. With the sledge and horse, however, matters were more difficult, for the former had got fixed under the ice, and the horse, with the instinct of self-preservation, just showed his nose above water. There was much lugging and hauling, shouting and halloaing, on the part of our men to get the poor animal out, and ultimately a success was made of the effort. But the sledge was smashed quite beyond repair, and perforce we had to abandon it. Room had to be made for Gaskell, therefore, and this was accomplished by half emptying one of the baggage-sledges, panniering the baggage on the spare horse's back.

Right once more, we continued our journey, all of us considerably more careful now, and ultimately we got down on to the ice, and felt safer. The little river Armeul was not more than a furlong wide, and wound tortuously through gaps in the hillsides. In summer it was simply a torrent, and going up-stream was simply going up-hill, for we were to follow its course right up into the mountains. We went along at a jog-trot, varied by spells of walking, and so the day passed. Night came on, and with the blinking stars we endeavoured to get a little sleep; but this we speedily realized was quite out of the question, for the fearful bumps and jolts which were occasioned by the deep holes in the road made it a difficult matter to hang on, let alone to repose. In that faint starlight it was a weird proceeding to be travelling over this uneven surface; to dimly see your horse suddenly disappear before your eyes, and then to feel yourself sink down as if you were going into the bowels of the earth, only to be brought up with a crash at the bottom of the hole, sufficient to shake every bone in your body. Then, the next second, up would go the horse on the other side of the hole, struggling, kicking, and straining, with snow flying from its hoofs in all directions, and with you, hanging on to the reins with the tenacity born of the love of self-preservation, nearly falling out of the back of the sledge. Well into the night we rounded a huge cliff, which, towering up, blotted out the firmament, and left only a small circle of the dark blue sky, and sighted, away ahead, a light winking solemnly. Simultaneously we all raised a shout, for it was the light of the hut of the first stage, and even the horses, after their eighty versts' toilsome pull, seemed to recognize it. Pace was put on, and in a few minutes our caravan drew up at the side of the river, before the hut.

Now we were roughing it with a vengeance. The hut was a small affair, built of logs and mud, its roof of twigs and hay, and with no vestige of comfort within. It was simply a shelter, but we were glad of that. After the horses had been unhitched and hobbled, one of our men started a roaring fire with some fuel which we had brought with us, and which was made outside in the open. An iron tripod was erected, kettles and saucepans hung over, and we prepared for our meal. The custodian of the hut, a decrepit old man, smothered in the filthiest sheepskins that ever I clapped my eyes on, busied himself on our behalf. It was easy to see the pleasure which animated this poor old fellow, who for days, and sometimes a week at a stretch, never saw a human face, and who had no more chance of getting food than was given him by the miners going to or coming from the mines, or by the fish he could catch through a hole made in the ice.

Cold as it was, the fire outside the hut was warm enough for anything. Some of our men, intent on not doing things by halves, had disappeared in the forest with their hatchets, and presently we heard the clump, clump, of the steel against the tree-trunks, and soon we had whole trees blazing and crackling on the river-bank, while the light cast up by this huge bonfire spread red and white across the frozen river to light up with its lambent glare the façade of the cliffs on the opposite bank. It was a wild-looking crowd we made, seated around on the hay bags, with feet almost in the crackling embers, furs still on, and eating almost ravenously the soup which had been prepared in the huge saucepan. How delicious it was, although it was eaten out of rough wooden bowls, with no cutlery save our hunting-knives, and with our fingers as forks! What matter if we licked our fingers, if we gnawed the bones, or were even guilty of wiping our mouths on our sleeves! Pocket-handkerchiefs had been given the go-by some time before, and this part of Siberia was no place for ceremony. We ate, and we drank heartily, meanwhile that the fire blazed, and roared, and lit up in fantastic light and shadow the motley crowd around it.

The hut would not hold more than four, but, unfortunately for our peace, it was alive with vermin. We brought in plenty of straw and hay from the sledges and spread it on the earth floor, and then, wrapping ourselves in our shoubas, sought sleep. For our employés there were the sledges, and in these they slept.

It was still dark when Schultz awoke us and intimated that it would be better to get on. A glance at our watches showed that it was 6 a.m., and though we would fain have had more sleep, the necessity of the case knew no delay. The second stage threatened to be even more difficult than the first, for we were informed in several places the ice of the river was broken owing to the water passing away underneath, and there would be much trouble in order to get through to the next hut, eighty versts away. I must confess that when I staggered out of the hut in the bitter cold air, I felt anything but happy or cheerful. The romance of the thing was all right, and the experience one to be always remembered. Its actuality, however, was the sort of thing to make a man cross or even despondent. Outside, the fire had dwindled down to a few glowing embers and wreaths of smoke; the stars had gone out, and a faint mist was in the atmosphere. I stood there for a moment, and as I did so heard two or three long-drawn howls. Dogs, I thought. I asked Schultz, who was by my side, what it was.

"*Vulka*," he said, and at the time I did not know that he meant wolves.

We shambled off in the darkness, Schultz leading the way with a lantern, and soon the hut, distinguished alone from the darkness by the tiny fire in front of it, grew fainter and fainter to our vision as we progressed, and soon a bend in the river obliterated it entirely, and we plunged on into the darkness. Day came imperceptibly—the grey creeping over the hill-tops ahead of us and gradually suffusing the horizon. Then a few glints of gold on the very tops of the mountains, the reflection of which shed roseate hues upon smaller and more insignificant hilltops. This glowing light, heralding the arrival of the sun, caused the mountain crests to assume most grotesque shapes. One stood out like a gigantic frog, another was like a man's face, a third was like an alligator, and so on. With the rising sun the mist cleared off, and we were able to traverse the ice at a better pace. But soon the road became next door to impassable. Here and there the river ice had broken in, and the water, freezing again, left but a thin coating, which was quite insufficient to bear the weight of our caravan. This necessitated the dragging, one by one, of the sledges over the hummocky ice, or up on the pathway which was here and there formed on the river-bank, where the cliffs did not run sheer. At midday we encamped on a small plateau by the side of the river, built our fire, made more soup and more tea. It was cheerful, at any rate, to note the good humour which characterized all our men. No matter how difficult was the passage of the ice, they all went at it like bricks, and when one way failed they tried another. Schultz, a gigantic fellow of six feet four, or thereabouts, was ever to the fore, hauling and tugging, or with his huge pick breaking away the impeding ice ahead.

To record the details of our journey forward would be but reiteration. Thoroughly exhausted, we arrived at our second stage late in the afternoon, and put in eight hours' good solid sleep. On the third day we arrived at the headwaters of the Armeul, where the river was only a few feet wide, and where the springs feeding it burst from the rock, but now hung masses of huge icicles. There was a pathway through the forest to the eastward, and over this we had to go to our destination. This pathway had been formed by the miners cutting their way through with the hatchet. The trees were so close together that, although it was day when we entered, once inside the wood, things were almost as black as night. Now and again, as we progressed, we caught sight of animals flitting about the underwood of the forest, but with all the nonsense about wolves knocked out of us by travel, we gave them no heed, save for an occasional rifle-shot which Scawell sent after them.

On the afternoon of the fourth day we

arrived at the top of the first range of mountains, and below us lay a deep valley through which the tiny stream known as the River Isinsoul wound its course, and upon whose banks was the property which formed our destination. Right ahead of us, towering up almost perpendicularly, rose the final range of the Syansk Mountains, the barrier between Russia and China, and now not more than five miles away.

Our descent into the valley was rapid and exciting. The road was every bit as bad as it had been on the river, and was, moreover, precipitous. Horses stumbled, fell, and rolled over into the snow. Once I was shot out of the sledge, and my feet, catching in the reins, I was dragged along a considerable distance before my horse could be stopped. Scarcely a minute after my accident, Asprey was thrown violently out, and his head, striking a projecting tree-trunk, he was knocked nearly insensible. A little later one of the baggage-sledges overturned, and we had the glorious spectacle

GOLD-MINING APPARATUS ON THE UPPER YENESEI.

[*To face page* 192.

of our goods and chattels flying in all directions down the hill.

Passing through the fringe of the forest we came out upon the slopes of the valley, and now could clearly see, on the banks of the river below us, traces of the work of man in the shape of huts and long aqueducts, but all covered in snow and silent as the grave. At length we were fairly down in the bed of the valley and making our way along the course of the Isinsoul, hoping to reach our destination before darkness fairly set in. What a shout we gave when, just as the sun was sinking over the mountains to our back, Schultz announced that we had reached the edge of the property! Huge mounds of earth, the tailings of the washeries, but covered in deep snow, lay scattered all around. A few dismantled huts, some heaps of logs here and there, the traces of an abandoned washery, all looking desolate and forlorn underneath their snowy covering. Three versts more and we came in sight of some huts away up on the hillside, which we learned were to form our headquarters for the next two or three weeks. A man came out of one of the huts and waved his hand. Schultz responded with a whoop that would have done credit to a North-American Indian, and the horses, scenting rest, sprung bravely forward. On we rattled and creaked, jerked and bumped, until with a simultaneous sigh of most intense satisfaction we drew up before the sluice-house of the mine. Our destination at last, after five and a half weeks' almost continual travelling from England!

CHAPTER XIV.

SIBERIAN GOLD-MINING.

It is not my intention to go into very intricate details regarding gold-mining in Siberia, but would rather give a few personal observations of what is undoubtedly a very interesting phase of Asiatic life, inasmuch as gold-mining in that country is very different to what it is in any other part of the world. The Minusinsk district, in which we were now located, though not by any means the richest in Siberia (that distinction being held by the mines of the Lena district, in the province of Yakutsk), is nevertheless looked upon as an extremely promising province. The richness of the Lena district is considerably counter-balanced by the high price of provisions, labour, and material there, and its inaccessibility. The Minusinsk district, on the other hand is the most remarkable in all Siberia for its cheapness, while transportation is fifty per cent. lower than on the Lena watershed. From Krasnoiarsk, where the trunk line of the Siberian Railway passes, there is steamboat communication in the summer with Minusinsk itself, and, as I have already said, the gold-bearing district extends from there southwards to Chinese territory.

The majority of the mine-owners in the district were, I found, of very humble origin, and it may be said, with the exception of one man, Kuznetsoff, not one works on a large scale, while the majority have started without initial capital whatever. The consequence of this is that the works are generally of a mean character. Machinery is of the most primitive order, and what there is is so badly and unscientifically made that in all cases some twenty per cent., and in many cases fifty per cent., of fine gold is lost. Hydraulicing is quite unknown, and the chemical process has never been tried thoroughly, the nearest approach to it being the fixing, on some of the Kuznetsoff mines, of amalgamating plates in the sluices.

Most of the mine-owners, being without initial capital, are forced at the onset to resort to tribute work, which is done by men who provide their own food, tools, and houses, and erect their own washeries. These men are given so many "archines" of land to work, and the gold obtained they sell to the mine-owner for from three to four roubles per "zolotnik" (about one-seventh of an ounce, Troy), the miner re-selling the gold to the Government at its current value, the price of the zolotnik varying from four and a half to five roubles. But the damage which is done to the property by tribute labour is enormous. The men work in gangs of three or four, burrow and scratch like rabbits here and there, and dump their tailings wherever it is most convenient to do so (frequently on new ground); so that before the whole of the mine can be worked out, the virgin alluvial has to be got out from under tons of débris. This improvidence on the part of the tribute workers naturally ruins mine after mine. The men are content to get a zolotnik per man per day, and in order to obtain this erect fast sluices, and put over an enormous amount of alluvial so as to get the big pieces, complacently letting the fine gold escape. One of the mines we saw during our stay had been worked for some forty years mainly by tribute labour, and the consequence was that although the property was by no means worked out (it extended some three and a half miles up a rich valley) it was impossible to make a profit out of it on account of the thousands of tons of tailings which encumbered the remaining portions of unworked ground. And this is no single instance. The Mining Department is continually hammering away at the mine-owners to exercise more system in their work, hinting broadly that not only are they losing themselves but that the Government suffers.

I have already said that the machinery used is of a primitive character. The tribute workers use the box-sluice, or "Long Tom." This is a wooden structure from twenty to thirty feet long, tapering from two feet at its top to one foot at the bottom. It is generally erected on the level of the stream, and, as most of the tributaries of the Yenesei have a very rapid current, the drop is pretty acute. There are no riffles or cross-pieces in the sluices to catch the fine gold, but an iron plate pierced with half-inch holes is set at the end, and through these holes the gold drops by its own weight into a shallower undercurrent sluice, where a slow stream of water carries away the lighter sand and leaves the gold exposed. The "Long Tom" constructed by the Siberians is, however, so unscientifically made that it would be hopeless to expect it to catch all the gold.

The machine of the mine-owner is a more

elaborate, but at the same time far from ideal structure. The sluice-house is built up over the stream, and usually contains three wide box-sluices, dropping one into the other, the last one being riffled with one or two bars. The length of the run would not be more, on the average, than forty feet, while the angle is such that the water flows in a perfect swirl from start to finish. At the back of the house, and above the sluice-boxes, an iron cylinder, pierced with half to three-quarter inch holes, is erected on a wooden axle. The cylinder tapers from one end to the other, and at its largest end a shoot is erected, under which the carts, which carry away the big boulders, can be backed. The cylinder is revolved by water power, carried along an aqueduct which varies in length according to the fall of the stream. Into the cylinder at its smaller end the auriferous sands are pitched, water at the same time being conducted upon it by pipes along the axle, and thus the whole mass is churned up. The boulders and stones which will not pass through the holes gradually roll down the declivity of the drum to its larger end, and thence into the shoot, while through the holes the fine sands containing the precious dust fall into the sluices below. At the shoot end, the collectors of the boulders carefully examine the stones for the presence of any nuggets; but, as a general rule, the wealth of the alluvial consists in the small pieces which pass through the holes. If the sluices were longer, and the angle so arranged that the water flowed smoothly and evenly over them, there would not be much to object to in this system, but the miners acknowledge that fully twenty per cent. of fine gold escapes into the tailings, without endeavouring in the slightest to remedy the defect. Amalgamating plates, or even a judicious use of mercury, would prevent much of this loss, but these appliances are almost entirely ignored.

It is the very cheapness of labour and material in the Minusinsk gold region which is accountable for the absence of modern mining machinery, and the unscientific method of washing. In nineteen cases out of twenty the present gold-miners have been washers, who, having at some time or other hit upon an unclaimed gold-bearing spot, have applied to the Mining Department for permission to work it. Instead of getting capital they have invited tribute workers to extract the gold, until, after a few years of rigid economy they have saved enough money to erect a machine and can continue the work by ordinary labour. Meanwhile, the value of the mine has been woefully depreciated by the methods of the tribute workers.

The alluvial deposits of the Minusinsk district do not vary to any great extent in richness; the average being generally under one ounce to the ton. This is, compared with alluvial working in Australia, Africa, and California, rather poor, but the cheapness of everything must be taken into consideration as a big set-off. Men cost in the winter twelve to fifteen roubles (25s. to 31s.)

per month, and in the summer eighteen to twenty roubles (38s. to 42s. 6d.) per month. Wood is abundant, and costs nothing except the labour of cutting it. Provisions are likewise very cheap; bread, meat, eggs, hay, and such like necessities being cheaper in the Minusinsk valley than in any other part of Siberia.

Mining material and provisions are generally carried from the townships to the mines during the winter, so that the ice on the rivers can be taken advantage of. The cost of transport is twenty-five kopecks ($6\frac{1}{2}d.$) per pood per 100 miles. The pood equals 36 lbs. 6 ozs. English. The Minusinsk mining region covers about three hundred square miles, so that an approximate estimate of the cost of transport can be made.

One of the great features about the district is its great suitability for hydraulic working. Water is everywhere abundant, and the cost of erecting a modern hydraulicing plant would be undoubtedly very much cheaper than in any other gold district. The alluvial deposits are eminently suited for such work, and where virgin ground is touched, all things being equal, hydraulicing ought to increase the profits on the Russian methods by twenty-five to thirty per cent. For purposes of comparison, the Russian gold-seeker looks to a profit of twenty-five per cent. on whatever small capital expended. With labour-saving machinery, and the ability to tackle five or six times as much stuff in the summer as under the Russian system, it stands to reason that the initial cost of machinery would soon be wiped out and the increased percentage of profit obtained.

To show how arduous the Russian method of working is, there is one mine in the Minusinsk valley which has been worked for upwards of thirty years. The claim is three miles long by a quarter of a mile wide. During the thirty years an average of thirty men per year have been employed in gold washing, and the mine has already yielded gold to the value of about £400,000. Even after thirty years, yet one-third of the claim is virgin soil. With hydraulicing methods, and with no more men employed, the mine could have been exhausted in two or three summers.

There is no working for quartz gold in the Minusinsk region, and but very little in any other part of Siberia. There *are* quartz deposits, and the alluvial strata shows indication of the proximity of reefs. Want of capital, want of machinery, and lack of enterprise have, however, prevented the exploitation of this profitable branch of the gold-mining industry so far.

We were very much struck to find the enormous number of mines the owners of which were most anxious to get rid of them, although their gold-books showed that even under primitive conditions the various properties were showing handsome profit. It was strange to interview sheep-skin clad moujiks who had rich mines to sell, and who could not work them themselves simply by reason of their lack of capital or their ignorance as to the right way to go about the work. Fancy prices were asked at first, only to come down to an "old song," when we evinced no anxiety to buy.

Most of the worst features of gold-mining in any part of the world are to be seen in Siberia. Stealing and murder are of frequent occurrence, in spite of the large number of Cossacks which are employed to keep law and order. One great grievance of the miners in the Syansk Mountains is the stealing propensity on the part of the workmen, and the open dishonesty which one owner shows to the other. For instance, an owner will give his tribute workers, say, three and a half roubles per zolotnik of gold obtained. The tribute worker, however, hands over only a portion of what he finds, reserving the remainder for sale to a neighbouring miner, who will probably pay him four and a half roubles for it. Thus many of the miners prefer to work on the tribute system instead of getting an ordinary wage. Even the paid labourer steals his master's gold, to sell it to some neighbouring miner; but as each owner adopts precisely the same methods, and the utmost secrecy has to be maintained, duplicity is rampant all over the fields.

Various prices were asked for mines, from 50,000 roubles down to 20 roubles. Another plan freely offered is to rent an existing mine with option of purchase, the rent demanded by the owner varying from 200 to 300 half-imperials per pood of gold obtained. The half-imperial is $7\frac{1}{2}$ roubles paper currency, and equals approximately 16s. The value of a pood of ligature gold ranges from £1700 to £2200, the general average value being about £2000.

On the whole, while the Russian mine-owner may make, what is to him, a fortune out of gold-mining, the general prospect for foreign capital in the Syansk Mountains is not a very alluring one if the workings are continued on Russian ideas. There is plenty of gold in the district, but an enormous quantity of alluvial has to be moved before it can be won, and while this removal yields a profit to the

Russian owner, that profit would perhaps be wiped out if on top of the ordinary expenses such as those to which the Russian miner is subjected are placed director's big fees, large salaries for engineers, and other expenses which are generally incidental to British gold-mining companies. The men who have made fortunes in Siberia are the owners who have in the first instance taken an active part in the working, and have generally superintended the business themselves. The overseers, engineers, and suchlike officials work for salaries which would not buy the clothes of similar individuals in Western Australia or South Africa. One of the mines we visited, belonging to the Kuznetsoff group, had a responsible manager at a salary of 1500 roubles (£160) per annum. It would, however, be in buying groups of mines, and by working with enormous numbers of men and with the most modern machinery, hydraulicing, or otherwise, that the Siberian gold-fields might be made to pan out as profitable and with far less risk than that usually

TRIBUTE WORKERS IN THE SVANSK GOLD-MINES.

[*To face page* 208.]

experienced in the hunt for the precious metal in other countries. To work on a small scale one must adopt the Siberian methods, and the foreigner's chance of doing this at a profit is not enhanced by the fact that he is likely to be cheated and robbed far more than his Russian compeer.

CHAPTER XV.

LIFE AT THE MINE.

ALTHOUGH somewhat rough and primitive, our quarters at the mine were by no means uncomfortable. There were in all four log houses, tolerably large, two of which were for the workmen, and the other two for ourselves. Of course there was not the slightest attempt in the way of luxury; rough wooden walls, dirt floors, hard benches for beds, a board resting on a tree-stump for a table, and an iron stove, with several feet of piping, as our heating accommodation. A little ingenuity on our part, however, soon rigged up things in businesslike fashion. Some roughly made shelves were requisitioned, and with other boarding and the assistance of Schultz we made a tiny office, and spread around our books in ostentatious display. We made up our beds with the spare clothing we possessed, and that was ample. We provided a tablecloth out of a huge towel which was fished from the bottom of Asprey's trunk, and we decorated the walls with various pictures cut from old comic papers. We got one of the men to go into the forest and bring us several armsful of fir foliage, and thus, after an hour or two's hard work was done we had succeeded in completely altering the appearance of the interior of our quarters, and to its general improvement.

It was a sight to see the manner in which our men hogged in together in one hut. Instead of doing the slightest in the way of improving their situation, they simply laid around on the floor, as closely as possible to each other, in order to get warmth, and covered with their sheepskins. By the regulations laid down by the Mining Department we had to allow each man so many poods of meat per week, so many candles each, tea, butter, and cabbage. We had brought with us three frozen oxen, four sheep, and forty poods of cabbage, and the task of weighing out the various portions to each man was by no means a light one, which, as it devolved upon me, I speedily found. As well as providing the men with food, we had to supply them with certain portions of clothing, should they require them, writing off against their wages the cost of such articles. It is astonishing how minutely the Russian Government goes into these matters, providing a schedule of prices which shows how much a pair of boots or articles of clothing must be charged the workmen. If nothing else, the authorities fully protect the peasants from extortion on the part of the mine-owner.

For several days we did little else but get things shipshape. Wood had to be cut in order to provide firing. Several of the men were kept hard at work cutting pathways through the deep snow down to the river-bed. The stream, as a matter of fact, was solid ice nearly to the bottom, and only near the sluice-house, where the channel had been cut deep, could we find much water. Our first endeavour was to discover whether or not in the tailings, which had been idly thrown away after nearly thirty years of washing, there was sufficient gold to warrant its exploitation on European plans. To the reader it may seem rather incongruous that we should have to conduct an inspection as this in such weather; but time was pressing. Whatever was done in the district had to be finished before the ice broke. If this occurred, the transportation of men and provisions from Minusinsk to the gold-fields would be delayed until the summer roads were ready, which, by the way, rarely happened before the beginning of July.

It is not my intention to weary the reader with a detailed description of our work, conducted as it was under such difficulties of weather and with but scant assistance from the local officials. The statements which were made by one and the other were so conflicting that the greatest care had to be exercised, while we had not been long in the district before we found that the gentle art of " salting " was not entirely unknown to the apparently guileless Siberian. What freezing work it was to be from daybreak to sundown on the banks of the river, pan-washing the pay dirt, which had to be got out from under tons of ice and snow, and dug out bit by bit with light steel picks! We commenced at the bottom of the mine, and worked gradually up by burrowing in through the snow to the scene of summer operations, and there only to find the earth frozen as hard as granite, necessitating occasional blasting and much hard and unprofitable labour.

The particular mine we were on, during the whole course of its existence, had been mismanaged to a terrible degree. It had been worked for the most part by tribute labour, and, in consequence, the richest parts of it were encumbered with tons of débris which would all have to be removed before the virgin alluvial could be got out. Frequently we had to work with snowshoes on, for some portions of the mine, where drifts had occurred, were under ten to fifteen feet of light snow. Snowshoeing at the best of times is a laborious undertaking, but to work with them on is a feat which requires some patience and a tolerable amount of agility.

One of our little experiences of snowshoeing was amusing, as well as being somewhat uncomfortable. Desiring a sample from the head of the mine, I had gone out with Gaskell and two of the men. The men were loaded up with picks, bags, shovels, and other mining paraphernalia, and, being more expert on the "skis" than we, soon outstripped us. It took us nearly an hour to do a little over a mile, for, what with frequent falling, our progress was one of labour and confusion. Snowshoes have a happy knack of sliding away from you when you least expect them, so that you come down with a thump on your back, and bury yourself up to the armpits in snow. No matter how you struggle, it is impossible to get up again, for the long shoes prevent that. The only thing is to unstrap the shoes, kneel on them, gradually insert one foot and then the other into the straps, and then by an equilibristic effort assume the perpendicular. The slightest want of balance and over you go again. The snow affords no foothold, for you sink into it the moment the shoes are off.

The spot from which we desired the sample was reckoned to be one of the richest portions of the mine. It was a tunnel cut into the river-side, but which was now completely covered with snow, so much so, in fact, that we could not even see the entrance. Our men, Merkoff and Nikeveroff, set to work spading out the snow, and gradually got to the tunnel entrance. Merkoff was in advance of his companion when, with a suddenness which made us gasp with astonishment, he disappeared completely from sight. Where he had gone none of us knew. The snow before us showed no trace of his disappearance, for there was no hole. Presently, however, we saw a hand come up through the snow and wave about frantically. In another second the whole bank on which we were standing, gave way with a rush, and down we went, snowshoes, picks, shovels, bags, candles, and everything in one confused heap, sliding and slipping some twenty or thirty feet below the level.

It was some time before we sorted ourselves out and got over the shock of our descent. We then found ourselves in a narrow gallery supported by beams, and which ran for some considerable distance into the earth. For a minute or two we could only sit and laugh, for our entrance of the tunnel had been highly successful if somewhat precipitous. The floor of the gallery was covered with ice, formed by the oozing of water through the bank, and for some time it was impossible to get at the alluvial owing to the excessive hardness of the ice flooring, which we were compelled to break with hammers. Strangely enough, although we had all got down so cleverly, none of us gave a thought as to how we were to get back. The samples obtained, this difficulty at once presented itself, and we could only gaze at each other blankly.

We were twenty or twenty-five feet below the level of the snow, and it was a matter of impossibility to think of climbing to the top of that fleecy substance. There was only one thing to do, and that was to batten the snow as hard as possible and to get up inch by inch to the surface. This was a long and laborious undertaking, and occupied us well into the afternoon, but ultimately Merkoff reached the top, and, his snowshoes having been thrown after him, he was able to stand up. Then the samples, by aid of rope, we got up, and eventually we all managed to get out of the hole.

The next thing to do was to get the samples back to the camp, a distance of a mile. Each was as much as one man could carry, provided that the roadway was hard. The weight of one, however, on Merkoff's back, sent the snowshoes so deep that it was impossible for him to move. We tried various ways, but none succeeded until it was decided to form a temporary sledge of the snowshoes, and for one of the men to drag the bags in this manner to the camp. At the time we did not think, when we gave up the shoes so cheerfully and sat down in the snow in order to prevent going in deeper, how we were ourselves going to get back to the camp. We formed the sledge by tying the shoes together, then fixed the bags and tools on top of them, and away went Merkoff, with Nikeveroff behind, crawling on his hands and knees, and giving the improvised sledge an occasional push. Gaskell and I attempted to walk. We might as well have tried walking on the sea. Every effort landed us deeper in the snow. There was only one way and that was to go down on all fours and wriggle along as best we could. Only then could we make progress by carefully beating down the snow as we went, to put the whole length of the arm down in one place, and drag the body after with a squirming motion. That mile was one of the hardest miles I have ever travelled, for darkness was falling when we came in sight of the huts. In spite of the cold, we were sweating with the labour, and to add insult to injury, our companions came down on the bank and howled with laughter as we progressed inch by inch along the surface of the snow.

A little incident like this will give some idea of the difficulties under which we worked. Another stumbling-block was the inability to wash the pay-dirt with ordinary water. Close by the sluice-house we had a huge iron cauldron suspended over a roaring fire. One man was kept continually employed dumping in snow, while another was ladling out buckets of hot water. The process was then to dump so many poods of earth on the wash-table and to break it up by continual basting with hot water. The washer (who stood on the table, and with his rake or wooden shovel kept the mass in motion) frequently got frozen to the wood, in spite of the fact that the water which flowed around his feet had only a few seconds before been thrown boiling hot on the dirt.

During our stay we were able to make several little excursions to neighbouring mines, and with the exception of one or two we found a shocking want of system everywhere. In the best-conducted gold-fields the disposal of the tailings is always a matter of grave moment, but in Siberia it is one of the least considerations until it is too late, and the property is ruined. There is, however, some hope that the future may be better, for the St. Petersburg Department, being now brought into closer contract with Siberia by means of the railroad, intends to formulate a better system of inspection, which, provided Siberian miners will only endeavour to look at matters in a broader spirit, should increase the revenue considerably.

A pleasing feature in connection with mining in Siberia is made by the little courtesies which one owner extends to the other. Thus we were continually receiving invitations to dinner at some mine or the other, and would drive over in our sledges to be welcomed literally with open arms by the rough but hospitable miners, to be kissed on both cheeks, and to be liberally supplied with everything the owner possessed in an eating way. Very pleasant indeed were these little functions, for, out of touch of anything like civilization, the grotesque customs which obtain in the towns of " dress " went to the winds, and the Siberian appeared for what he really was. There was perhaps a little bit too much drinking, and at times a want of manners which jarred unpleasantly, still one could not help but appreciate the hospitality which was extended to us, rough as it was. It was gratifying on those evenings after we had gone through the long dinner which is invariably the rule in Russian houses, to sit around and listen to the harmonica and to watch, between the puffs of our cigarette smoke, some big-booted miner going through that extraordinary dance made famous by the Little Russians. Considering what a clumsy, heavy, and ungainly lot the Russians generally are, one can scarcely associate them with the graceful mazurka, a dance of which they are passionately fond and perform creditably.

These visits of ours to neighbouring mines tended much to take away the monotony of our three weeks' stay in the mountains, and we had the pleasure, too, of receiving in our own camp the mine-owners who would pay us return visits. They had a happy way, some of them, of bringing whole cargoes of vodki, cigarettes, meat, vegetables, and, in short, everything deemed necessary for the occasion. Every man would lend his hand at the culinary arrangements; songs and dances interspersing various items of the menu; while, to add to our enjoyment, our own men would range up outside the hut and sing with lusty voice one of those peculiar national songs, the cadence of which once heard can never be forgotten.

CHAPTER XVI.

A TRIP INTO CHINA.

WITH the frontier of China so close, what was more natural than that the desire should spring up within me to penetrate, at any rate a little way, into that mysterious country? So far as I knew, and could gather, no European had yet crossed those mountain ranges into the valley of the Upper Yenesei, which runs between the Syansk range and the eastern slopes of the Altai.

The delimitation of the boundary-line between Russia and China is one of those ludicrous things which only the wily Muscovite knows so well how to manage. Maps showed the boundary to run along the tops of the Syansk range, yet when I asked where was

OUR CAMP IN THE MOUNTAINS. [*To face page* 224.

the actual frontier-line, not a man in the Minusinsk valley could tell me. Amongst the officials the idea of a frontier seemed to be a huge joke, and, penetrating deeper into the subject, the solution of the mystery was simply this : that the southern slopes of the Syansk Mountains were as rich in gold as the northern, with the additional qualification that they were less exposed to the rigour of the winter, and that the Russians coveted the district. In consequence of this, and mainly owing to the lax attitude of the Chinese Government, Siberian miners had penetrated beyond the geographical frontier, had opened mines, and were in quite a flourishing condition. The Russian officials meanwhile " winking the other eye," and accepting the gold from the miners just as if it had been obtained from mines well within the border. Not only that, but enterprising miners had conceived the idea of penetrating even further towards the Altai range, which is well within Chinese territory ; but owing to the treachery of some busybody the news of their programme reached official ears in Pekin. Complaints were lodged at St. Petersburg, and the diplomatic shuffle began.

Said the Russian, "Where is the frontier? If you know it to be at the top of the Syansk Mountains, why did you not prevent Russians from coming over into your country and operating?"

Said the Chinaman, "North-Western China is practically uninhabited. We cannot keep officials all along that frontier to prevent your people coming in!"

Said the Russian, "Well, what are you going to do? Our people have been there, have established themselves, and it would be a shame to oust them now. Suppose we arrange it this way. Let them go on working just as they are, and we will promise that no more Russians shall open mines in your country."

To this Pekin agreed. No surveillance was or is kept, and the consequence is that gradually, but nevertheless surely, the Russian is creeping into North-Western China. On the very top of the Syansk Mountains, and quite half a mile over the boundary line, as marked geographically, I have myself seen no less than five shafts sunk at spots which are supposed to lead to quartz veins.

The ludicrousness of the situation is shown by the fact that the officials of the Russian Government are well aware of the whole business, as it is necessary that before a man can prospect he must lay before the Department exact details as to the locality in which he intends to operate.

Having some interest in geography, I made some searching inquiries into this matter, but, as I have hinted, everywhere I was met with evasive replies. One of the chief officials whom I met, said, in so many words, that the frontier was where you could not find a Russian, and then burst into a hearty laugh.

Beneath this supposed nonchalance, however, it is easy to detect the trace of Imperial designs. "It is absurd," said one official, "to call the top of the range the frontier. The natural boundary is of course, the Yenesei River, which, as you see, after winding through the mountains, curves round in a semicircle to the mountains again." Then, emphatically, "It *must* be Russian."

Again, I had an interesting conversation with a Russian official on the subject of the railway. The Mongolian map was spread before us, and I traced from memory the course the line would take over the north-eastern Gobi. "Do you think you will have difficulty with the natives in this province?" I asked. My official friend simply winked. "If we do," said he, "we have plenty of Cossacks to keep them in order; and if the Cossacks are once in they won't come out very soon. And," continued he airily, "of course that part of the country north of the line *must* eventually become Russian."

Recent events tend considerably to corroborate these statements. One very singular fact about the matter is that the maps issued by the Russian Government to the officials close to the border do not show a single trace of the frontier-line. At present there is nothing to stop the slow but steady creeping of the Russian grey coats into Chinese Mongolia all along the frontier from west to east.

It was in order to find out more about this frontier business that I planned a little excursion to China, being aided and abetted by Seawell, who also had desires in that direction. We started out early one morning with one sledge, and with Schultz as our driver. For some distance the snow had been kept hard, and a decent road took us up the mountain-side. After an hour or two, however, the way got very precipitous, and perforce we had to abandon the sledge and continue our journey on snowshoes. Halfway up the mountain-side we passed though a dense forest, which obliterated, for the time being, all view of the surrounding country, and where it was terribly hard work pushing our snowshoes through the undergrowth which stuck out here and there through the deep snow. At length we got through the forest, and came out on the edge of a bluff which overlooked the whole surrounding country. The sight was one which no pen can describe.

Below us to the northward lay Siberia, a tumbled, mountainous country, which seemed to lie at our very feet—jagged masses of rock sticking out, cones of huge hills far below us, all silent, and white, and ghostly. Afar off we could just dimly see, by the aid of our field-glasses, the huts which formed our camp; beyond that, hills upon hills, clothed with fir, or pine, or birch, undulating away into space. To the south was a different scene, for here the mountains sloped away gently to a plain, and, singularly enough, here and there, instead of the great mass of white which was everywhere on the Siberian side, we detected patches of green and brown. We were some six thousand feet above the sea-level, and fleecy clouds at times swept around us, obliterating on one hand or the other the magnificent views which, as we stood, we drank in with keen enjoyment.

Our descent of the southern slopes of the Syansk was rapid and exciting. Only those who have travelled on snowshoes can realize what it means to go slithering down a slope with absolutely no prospect of stopping yourself except by falling backwards heavily. I am sorry to say, occasionally, and quite unintentionally, we did stop ourselves, and by this method. It had taken us the best part of a day to get up the northern heights. It took us less than an hour to get down three thousand feet on the southern side. To our surprise we found here not more than a few inches of snow, and we were safe in taking off our snowshoes in order to continue our journey, trailing them behind us in order to leave a mark in the snow which would show our direction for the return journey. Before us stretched almost a level plain, but, tapering away off to the right, we could dimly discern the blue tops of the Altai Mountains, in the intervening distance being occasional clumps of trees of much the same character as those on the Siberian side. Progressing on, we now and again came to patches of brown earth or grass with no more snow on them than might be seen in England at midsummer. This complete transition from the terrible cold, snow, and ice on the other side of the mountains was a revelation to us. The very air was warmer—in fact, it seemed as if in the space of a few hours we had jumped from the middle of an Arctic winter into spring. We doffed our fur caps and pelisses, carrying them over our shoulders, and weighty they seemed now, for the walking brought the sweat out.

We had paused by the side of a stream which was brawling away merrily, as innocent of ice as ever one could conceive, and, while sitting on its bank, partaking of a nip of spirit, Scawell espied, away across the plain, a tiny wreath of smoke curling upwards. Our first thought was that this probably came from one of the Russian mines which we had heard of, and so, anxious to see how the operations were being conducted, we immediately set out towards it.

An hour's stiff walk brought the smoke much nearer, and we were able to see that instead of a mine we were coming upon an encampment of some sort. Through our field-glasses we could see several black tents, and around them some strange animals, which in the distance we could not make out, although it was clear they were neither horses nor oxen. Another half-hour and we were within hailing distance of the encampment, and saw that instead of Russians we had fallen in with some of the natives of the province, the aboriginal Syots. The strange animals, we now perceived, were reindeer. We held a little council of war as to what to do, and the outcome of it was to go on and see all we could.

Strange-looking beings appeared before their tents, shouting excitedly as we approached.

They were attired in the most grotesque fashion, huge skins forming one garment from head to foot. Their faces were of the true Mongolian type, and far more hideous than the Chinese. The eyes were big, oblique to a degree, cheek bones very high, and the skin almost black. One of these individuals came running towards us and addressed us in Russian, and the words, "*Morjna kopeet saable, koreshee saable*," gave us a hint. We had heard that the Syots are sable-hunters, and what they had said was a request to know if we had come to buy good sables. With nothing else to do, under the circumstances, we assented, and entered the encampment. One of the men, the chief evidently, conducted us to a tent which we entered with the gravity and solemnity due to the occasion. The tent was a primitive affair—merely undressed skins stretched over a few poles which tapered up to a point like the tepee of the red man. There was nothing inside except a few skins scattered over the earth of one corner, and which probably formed the resting-place of the inhabitant.

Our host, in broken Russian, made references to tobacco, tea, sugar, and gunpowder. Had we brought them? He had magnificent sables he would give in exchange—all the time that we, in the first novelty of our discovery, scarcely realized what it all meant. It was not long before we were surrounded by some twenty to thirty Syots, the dirtiest, ugliest crowd of humanity which it has ever been my lot to see. They looked at us curiously, evidently perceiving that we were not the same sort of Russians to which they had been accustomed. Their bewilderment at our intrusion became greater when it dawned upon them how little we knew of the Russian language, and I really began to fear that our hospitable reception would not end so peacefully as might have been anticipated at the outset. Scawell was for making tracks and getting out of it, and I, seconding his motion, rose to leave, but the chief bade us be reseated, and brought for our inspection some fifty skins, which even the unpractised eye could detect as being magnificent specimens of the sable. Had we got any tobacco, tea, gunpowder, or shot? Scawell had some cartridges, but these were useless for the weapons used by the Syots. They brought forward for our inspection one of the most unearthly looking guns, surely, that man has ever constructed. It was an arrangement consisting of a long piece of iron piping, plugged up at one end and fastened to the apex of a tripod; the tube had a hole bored about three inches from the plugged end, and this formed the touch-hole. Inquiries elicited the information that this is the usual instrument employed by the Syots in their capture of sables. How tenderly they caressed Scawell's Mannlicher! what wondering eyes they cast upon its mechanism! while my revolver astonished them. They could not conceive that so small a weapon could have such deadly effect as I told them. They asked us who we were and where we had come from;

but, think of it, ye Englishmen, these Syots knew of but two people — Mongolian and Russian!

Out there on the Chinese plain we sat in a tent endeavouring to explain to a crowd of swarthy aborigines that there was another country in the world called England, and that the whole of the earth's inhabitants did not consist entirely of Chinamen and Russians. It was interesting to hear from the lips of a Mongolian nomad his ideas of things in general. He had heard, he said, that afar off there lived a being called the " Ruski Imperator," who knew everything and could see everything. I asked the chief about the Emperor of China, but he looked in wonderment upon me, and it was clear he had never heard of him. I mentioned the name " Li Hung Chang," but again there was no recognition. How far-reaching and how omniscient must be the power of a king, therefore, who, like the Czar of Russia, could be known to a man who has never heard of the existence of a king of his own country!

Fortunately, I had brought with me several handsful of cigarettes, and these I distributed amongst the crowd, telling them at the same time that if they cared to come over the mountains to our encampment I would purchase their sables from them. Of money they knew nothing, but I elicted that an ordinary sable was worth half a brick of tea, which would weigh something about half a pound. A handful of gunpowder and a handful of small shot would be its equivalent, and that the Russian traders never gave more. When one considers that in Moscow and St. Petersburg a single sable skin of good quality will fetch £10 to £15 sterling, the fur-traders of Siberia must be doing a rather lucrative business.

We were anxious to get back, for there was not much daylight remaining, and impressed this upon our hosts, who good naturedly suggested that we should ride some of the reindeer back to the mountains—an offer which we gladly fell in with, as the tramp to the slopes was over three miles. I have ridden some curious animals in my time, but the reindeer with its long, shambling stride is something peculiar. One has to keep a sharp look out for his horns, which he occasionally throws back with a sweep sufficient to knock your head off if you are not careful. It was not a very enjoyable ride, I must admit, encumbered as we were with our snowshoes and our heavy pelisses, and we were glad when the slopes of the mountain had been reached and we were able to dismount and thank our strange conductors for their courtesy.

At sunset we scrambled to the top of the Syansk again, and commenced our descent into the snow and ice of Siberia. It was then that we fully realized the great change between these two climes. On went our pelts, our gloves, and our fur caps; then slither, slither, slither, we careered through the forest; down and down until we came out into the open again, and discovered our faithful Schultz comfortably asleep in the sledge and our poor horse, which had somehow got out of the track, buried up to its neck in the snow. Night had fallen when we reached the camp, well pleased with our day's excursion; for, if it yielded nothing else, it had given us an insight into the character of a people whose very existence is perhaps unknown to Europe.

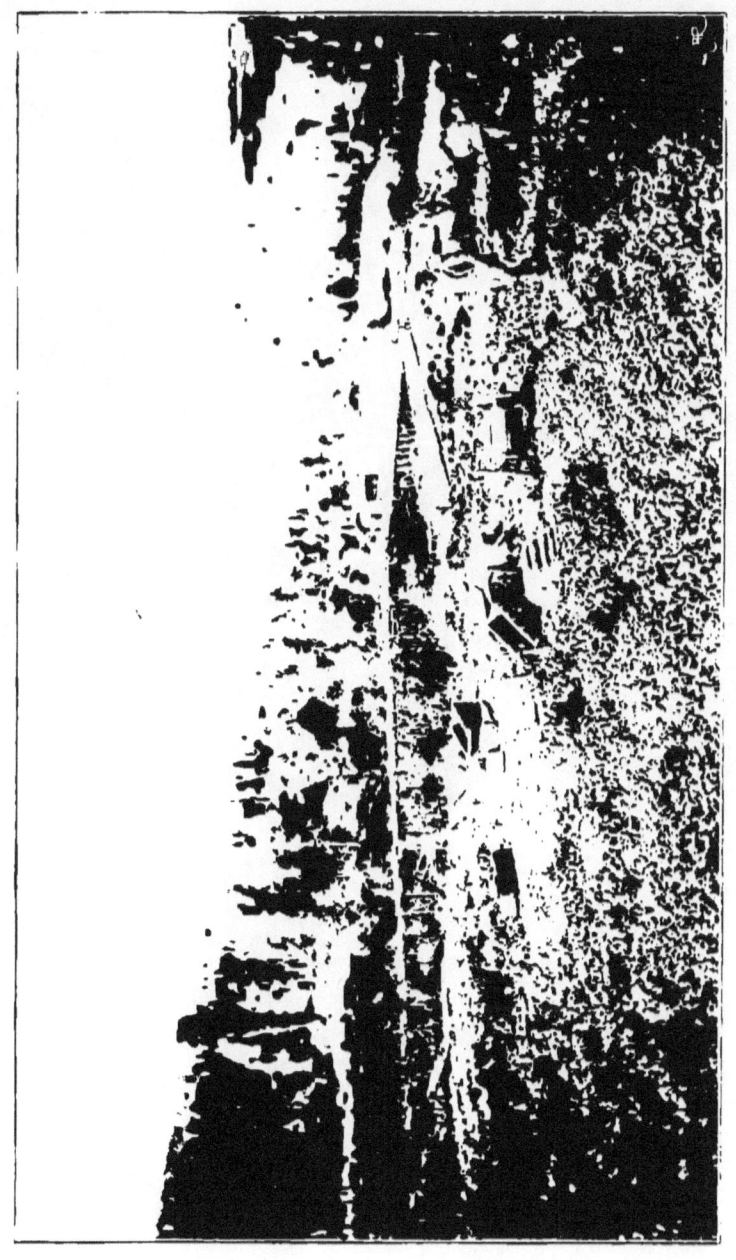

A GOLD-MINE ON THE TOP OF THE SVANSK MOUNTAINS.

[To face page 240.

CHAPTER XVII.

LOOKING WESTWARD.

For the next two weeks matters went on smoothly at our encampment. Days spent in labour, and evenings relieved by reading or the occasional visit from some neighbouring miner. How the world was getting on we had not the slightest idea, for, since leaving Moscow, we had received no word from those at home. We were now eagerly looking forward to the time when we should receive the first batch of correspondence. Arrangements had been made to forward our post from Minusinsk by horseback, and when, on the eventful morning, the news was brought up to our hut that the postboy was seen approaching, the excitement amongst us all was great. We almost fell upon the bundles of letters and newspapers which the faithful messenger had brought, sent work to the winds for the rest of that day, neglected our meals, and did nothing but devour the intelligence which cold print conveyed.

Signs were not wanting that it would not be very long before the break up of the winter would come about. The sun was daily getting warmer, and here and there the ice and snow were melting. The postboy told us that the River Armeul was thawing rapidly, and that if it was our intention to get back to Minusinsk on the winter road it would be necessary to speedily bring our operations to a close. There was, indeed, but little to detain us. Our expedition had been practically completed, and we needed now only the visit of the mining inspector to relieve us of the responsibility of our present position by handing over to him the enormous number of books and papers with which it had been necessary to burden ourselves in order to undertake our project.

Gaskell and I were to return straight to England, but Scawell and Asprey had other fish to fry, as they were to go further eastward into the provinces of Northern Manchuria. As the time approached for our departure our eagerness to be off became chronic. Visions of other lands and other peoples, of more cheerful surroundings, were ever before us—anything, now, to get out of this dreary waste of snow which for more than three months had enveloped us.

Our camp was the scene of some mild excitement when one day the Government inspector, attended by several servants and a whole string of horses, arrived. It was a great to-do, for he was an important-looking personage, very much epauletted and be-buttoned and extremely officious. His first duty was the inspection of our gold-book, and, as bad luck would have it, a couple of trivial mistakes had crept in, and within half an hour of the inspector's arrival we had to pay out fifty roubles as fines. It was a scene, too, later on in the day, when we called up our men for their pay and gave them their discharge. Criminals of the worst class though they were, we had got to like our little staff, and I think they in return reciprocated the feeling. Several of the men had made tremendous inroads on their wages in the matter of purchases of vodki and clothing, and one cheerful individual, after his sheet had been reckoned up, owed us a bit, although he humorously remarked that our chances of getting it were rather remote.

This was our last night in camp. On the morrow we were to depart on our westward journey, and to signalize the event our men got up an impromptu concert, which lasted well into the small hours, meanwhile that they drank themselves into a maudlin state.

Morning broke—just the same sort of morning as we had experienced during the whole time we had been in Siberia—cloudless, brilliant, white. Our little caravan was already ranged up outside the hut. The mining inspector was there to see us off. Asprey and Seawell had risen betimes, and had loaded us with messages to friends at home. It was a break indeed to part with those two good fellows who had been our boon companions for so many weeks in this cheerless land. The Siberians, I think, wondered why it was that we did not fall on each other's necks and kiss each other rapturously, as is the custom there. "You English have cold blood," said Schultz, "that you can part with your comrades like this!" For a hurried shake of the hand, "Good-bye, old boy, and good luck," was all. We ambled out of the camp, and then down the narrow pathway through the property. At the bend of the river we surmounted a small hill and looked back. Asprey and Seawell were on the roof of the hut, waving their scarves at us. The sound of a pistol-shot reached our ears. It was the parting salute, and we fired our revolvers in reply. Then we passed the brow and went down the great dip towards the Armeul, and we saw no more of our camp in the mountains, or of our comrades.

It took us five days to reach Karatuski, for it was now late in March, and the ice on the Armeul was breaking up right and left, rendering our passage one of extreme danger and difficulty. How welcome that little village seemed after the roughing-it we had experienced in the mountains! A man's appreciation of comfort depends considerably on where he has come from, and though Karatuski might be voted one of the most miserable spots on the face of the earth by he just fresh from Europe, it was a veritable city of plenty to us now.

From Karatuski to Minusinsk, and from Minusinsk to Atchinsk, with galloping horses night and day; for every morning saw the snow getting less and the great Yenesei cracking on all sides. Once, in the night, while travelling up the river, the ice broke under us, and we lost one of our horses. Only the fact that we were on the side, and not in the centre, of the river saved us from complete destruction. How welcome was the sound of the locomotive's whistle at the station of Atchinsk! and again when, as the cars rolled slowly in, what a link they seemed with the civilization of the West!

Day succeeded night and night succeeded day with us ever journeying westward. Familiar now were the names of the stations— Tigre, Kreveschokovo, Kainsk, Omsk, Kurgan, Chelabinsk. Only drifts of snow now in the mountain passes; buds to be seen on wayside trees; everything betokening the rapid approach of the Asiatic summer. Late one evening Gaskell awakened me from the nap into which I had fallen. The train was slowly grinding through a defile in the Ural Mountains. He looked at his watch. "In three minutes," said he, "we shall be in Europe." The minutes slowly ticked off, and then, rounding a bend, the sluggish train passed slowly the stone monument which separates Europe from Asia.

There is nothing more of moment to tell in connection with our journey to the Syansk Mountains. With the exception, probably, of the Captain Wiggins' expedition, we constituted, I think, the first English party to enter Siberia in order to inquire into the commercial resources of that vast country. The general impressions created by our visit I have endeavoured to set down as clearly as possible, and at a time when considerable attention is being directed towards Asiatic Russia it it possible they may be of some value. Travellers to Siberia hitherto have mainly consisted of those who have travelled through the country with the express desire of writing a book, and have confined themselves principally to the standard questions of the day; in which prisons, exiles, wolves, and bears form no inconsiderable part. The lasting impression which Siberia has upon me is that, while it is undoubtedly a land of promise, yet some few years must elapse before Europe can be brought into direct commercial contact with it. Anxious as the Government is to promote trade in Siberia, the distance and the primitiveness of the country will do much to delay matters; while, so far as Englishmen are concerned, the autocratic laws of the great White Czar can never be palatable. That there exists in Siberia a big field for the investment of foreign capital goes without saying, but whether Englishmen will grasp the opportunity is another matter. Ten years may see Siberia a far different country to what it is at the present time, and in this connection nothing will have tended more to remove the mystery and gloom of that great country than that magnificent State enterprise—the Trans-Siberian Railroad.

INDEX

Armeul, The river, 182, 191
Atchinsk, The town of, 107

Baraba steppe, The, 20

Chelabinsk, 1–13
Chulim river, The, 104
Colonization, Russia's scheme, 21
Criminal workmen, 170
Czar, The late, and the Siberian railway, 23

Emigrants' fares to Russia, 26
Emigrants' train, 27
English language in Russia, 15
Exiles, Condition of, 113

Frozen river, The, 72

Gobi desert, The, 228
Gold averages, 94
Gold-miners, Amusements of, 174, 222
Gold-miners, Siberian, 174
Gold-mining, Account of, 195
Gold-receiving depôts, 94
Grants of land to emigrants, 26

Irtish river, The, 19

Kansk, 69
Kara sea route, 114
Karatuski, Village of, 166

Khirghiz Cossacks, The, 55
Khirghiz horsemanship, 59
Khirghiz Kibitkas, or tents, 58
Krasnoiarsk, Population of, 112
Krasnoiarsk, The city of, 101, 110
Krasnoiarsk, The valley of, 108
Kurgan, 21

Machinery for gold-mining, 199
Merchandise, Siberian, 116
Millionaires of Tomsk, The, 87
Mining concessions, 97, 172
Mining laws, 98
Minusinsk, 133, 162
Moujiks, Siberian, 145

Nomadic tribes, 21

Ob, The station of, 74
Obi bridge, 69
Obi river, The, 69
Obi valley, The, 68
Omsk, 31

River sledging, 70
Russian Church, The, 32
Russian corruption, 102
Russian curiosity, 14
Russian incivility, 16
Russian railway travelling, Economy of, 128
Russian trade with Siberia, 51
Russian vigilance, 165

INDEX

Sable hunting, 235
Siberian cabmen, The, 40
Siberian food, 82
Siberian forest, A, 75
Siberian hospitality, 88
Siberian hotels, 43
Siberian posting stations, 45
Siberian railway station, Description of, 5
Siberian trains, Slowness of, 62
Siberikoff, M., 86
Sledging, 129, 139
Sledging, Dangers of, 153, 182
Sledging, Discomforts of, 186, 192
Snowshoeing, 215
Syansk mountains, 100, 181
Syots, The, 234

Tartar Steppe, The, 19
Tea-trade of Siberia, The, 116

Tigre, The station of, 74
Tom, The river, 86
Tomsk and the railroad, 52
Tomsk mining laboratory, The, 92
Tomsk, The city of, 76
Tomsk university, 87
Trans-Siberian Railway, Description of, 101, 120
Trans-Siberian Railway, Importance of, 126, 128
Transport, 202

Ural mountains, 1

Vladivostock, 24

Wiggins' expedition, 113

Yenesei, The valley of, 108
Yenesei river, The, 138

THE END.

www.ingramcontent.com/pod-product-compliance
Lightning Source LLC
Chambersburg PA
CBHW031338230426
43670CB00006B/371